Secrets from an Indian Kitchen

SECRETS FROM AN Indian KITCHEN

MRIDULA BALJEKAR

PAVILION

Dedication

For my two sisters and three brothers, in memory of all the childhood excitement and joy we were fortunate to share, and the abundance of good food, cooked with the freshest, finest ingredients and large doses of love by our loving mother.

First published in Great Britain in 2000 by
PAVILION BOOKS LIMITED
The Chrysalis Building
Bramley Road
London W10 6SP

An imprint of **Chrysalis** Books Group plc

Text © Mridula Baljekar
Photography © Ian Wallace
Design and layout © Pavilion Books Ltd.

Text designed by Andrew Barron & Collis Clements Associates

A CIP catalogue record for this book is available
from the British Library.

ISBN 1 86205 6196

Set in Swiss 721 light and Palatino
Originated by Anglia Graphics in Bedford

2 4 6 8 10 9 7 5 3

Printed and bound in Spain by Just Colour Graphic S.L, Barcelona

This book can be ordered direct from the publisher. Please contact
the Marketing Department. But try your bookshop first.

Contents

6 Introduction

16 Baghar – seasoning

30 Bhuna – stir-frying

46 Dum – steaming

64 Korma – braising

76 Tandoori – clay oven cooking

90 Kabab – kebab

104 Talana – deep-frying

116 Rice and Bread

136 Salads and Chutneys

146 Desserts

156 Suppliers

157 Index

Memories are made of spices

The aroma, colour and texture of a dish conjures up many vivid childhood memories for me. Intertwined within these experiences are the heady smell of pine trees, lush, green tea plantations, beautiful rivers and streams with an abundance of fresh fish and shellfish, wildlife galore, acres of paddy fields and orchards full of luscious fruit and vegetables.

Back in the foothills of the Himalayas, first in my grandmother's kitchen, then in my mother's, I spent many happy hours watching and helping. As a five-year-old girl, I was greatly attracted to the vivid displays of spices, lentils and beans, the smell of fresh mint and coriander, chillies of different colours and sizes grown in our back garden and, mostly, by the beautiful fish and shellfish brought in on a daily basis. Dazzling hues, warm textures and the glow of the wood fire created a most magical atmosphere. I loved to watch my grandmother's beautiful peaches-and-cream cheeks glow in the gentle fire in an otherwise dark and old-fashioned kitchen.

My childhood fascination for my grandmother's kitchen turned me into her little helper. I soon found myself mixing and blending the spices, marinating meat and poultry and helping to cook.
I thoroughly enjoyed spending time in her kitchen and playing with all the wonderful colours that also smelled delicious. It made a lasting impression. By the time I was eight years old, I had learned to recognize most of the spices and my palate was almost fully trained to detect ingredients in a cooked dish. I now realise that my grandmother had given me one of the greatest legacies and perhaps the most enduring gift I could ever have wished for. Little did she realise that my initial attraction was only for her 'Aladdin's cave' of a kitchen!

My mother's kitchen was a bit more modern. There I learned to appreciate the finer points of superbly cooked food and the intricacies of Indian cooking. She read widely about food and combined common sense with creativity to turn out fabulous meals for us. She used spices like an artist uses a palette, deftly mixing colours, textures and aromas, and taught me that food should be light and aromatic, that spices should enhance rather than mask the main ingredients.

I was also fortunate to have the guidance of our family cook who belonged to a rare breed of chefs known as the Mog cooks. They were in great demand in British households during the Raj and had the ability to produce superb food with a delicate balance between Indian and European cuisines. Very few British families stayed behind in the tea-growing north east once India gained independence and the Mog cooks were promptly employed by the local families.

I nourish nostalgic memories of festivals such as Diwali (the Hindu festival of lights) when my mother, along with our cook, would produce an amazing array of sweet and savoury food. The vast, colourful dishes were a real feast to the eye, each one distinctly different from the other in colour, texture, aroma and taste. But whether it was a sumptuous festive feast or a simple family meal, our family meal times were happy and each of us savoured every mouthful of my mother's loving creations.

I fondly remember my mother explaining Indian cooking techniques to me as she prepared amazingly delicious dishes, whether made with the simplest ingredient like a humble potato, or luxurious venison, which was my father's favourite meat. Even today I find it great fun to unravel the mystery of terms and techniques used in the world's various cuisines. It helps when cooking a dish to understand why a particular technique is being applied to that recipe; it is also beneficial to be able to imagine the colour, texture and flavour of the final product. Once you have this picture in mind, you will have a better understanding of why you need to do certain things in a particular way.

Cooking Indian food can be a joy if you have a clear idea of the various simple techniques used. In this book I aim to present each mouth-watering recipe through the techniques that are used to create it, and which are particularly interesting because they vary from region to region. Sometimes more than one technique is used in the same recipe, but I believe that cooking should be a relaxing and enjoyable pursuit, not a chore, so I have adapted the recipes to save that rare commodity called time, which my mother and grandmother did not have to worry about. These simplified but traditional cooking techniques make Indian dishes as easy and quick to prepare as any other. The Indian cuisine has for some time been misrepresented abroad under the more general term of 'Kari' or curry, meaning a sauce, which was established during the British rule over India. The collection as a whole offers the experience of eating a wide variety of true and authentic Indian dishes.

I firmly believe that cooking is an art where you can put your imagination to work without restrictions. Being able to adapt in order to create new recipes is half the fun of cooking, so I wish you happy cooking and happy eating!

Essential ingredients

Chillies

The fresh chillies used in Indian cooking are long and slim. Supermarkets often sell them as 'finger' chillies. Our fresh red chillies are the same as the Thai red chillies.

Fresh chillies can be frozen but should be used within a couple of months, otherwise the seeds inside tend to discolour. Use them straight from the freezer. Another way of preserving fresh chillies is in a screw-top jar in the fridge. Wash and dry the chillies thoroughly and remove the stalks after washing. Put the pods in the jar, seal and refrigerate for up to 4 weeks.

In most of the recipes in this book, you can remove and discard the seeds of the chilli if desired. This will give a slightly milder taste to the dish – it is the seeds of the chilli that contain the heat.

Garlic, ginger and onion

Among the fresh ingredients used in Indian cooking, the three typically recurring ones are ginger, garlic and onion, also known as the 'wet trinity'. Ginger and garlic can be bought in paste or purée form from most supermarkets but the home made version will have infinitely superior flavour.

If you do not want to prepare these each time you cook, simply purée a batch in your food processor, add a little cooking oil to prevent them from drying out, and store in a screw-top jar in the fridge. They will keep well for up to two weeks. As a general guide, a piece of 1 cm/½ in ginger will yield 1 teaspoon of finely grated or puréed ginger. Similarly, 1½ large garlic cloves will produce 1 teaspoon of pulp or purée.

Store fresh ginger and garlic in a cool, dry place and not in the fridge. Onions should be stored under the same conditions.

Flour

A range of flours are used to make breads, one of the staples of the Indian diet. The wheat flour used in Indian breads is known as atta. This is made by grinding the entire wheat kernel to a very fine powder. It is therefore full of nutrients, including a high proportion of roughage.

Other types of breads are made with semolina, rice flour, cornmeal, millet flour and besan (gram flour).

Ghee and oil

Until a few years ago, most Indian dishes were cooked in the clarified butter known as ghee, although some regions did traditionally use oil. Now, like the West, Indian people are aware of the dangers of consuming too much saturated fat. Apart from certain Mogul dishes for which ghee is essential, most of the day to day cooking is done in light vegetable, corn or groundnut oil.

I prefer to use sunflower, vegetable or soya oil in order to achieve that light and digestible nature of any dish.

Herbs

Coriander (cilantro) and mint are two of the fresh herbs most frequently used in Indian cooking. Both can be washed, chopped and frozen.

Coriander will keep well in the fridge for a week as long as you remove any yellow or brown leaves first. Wrap the roots in a double or triple thickness of wet kitchen paper and place the whole bunch, root side down, in a large plastic bag. Tie up the top of the bag and place in the fridge.

Every time you use the leaves, check the bunch carefully and remove any that are beginning to turn brown or yellow.

Paneer

Although paneer is generally referred to as Indian cottage cheese, it is more akin to curd cheese. When the curd cheese is made it is known as chenna and is used in many sweets and desserts.

Chenna, when pressed, becomes harder and is known as paneer. It can be cut into different shapes and used in both sweet and savoury dishes. Paneer is an important source of protein among the vegetarian population of India. It is available in some supermarkets, however if you can't find it, halloumi, the Mediterranean cheese, is a good substitute for savoury dishes.

If using halloumi, you will have to carefully adjust the salt content of the dish as it contains much more salt than paneer.

Rice

Rice has been grown in this part of the world since about 1900 BC. Among the different types of long-grain rice used, basmati is the most esteemed and is considered to be the king of all long-grain rice. The name basmati means 'full of fragrance': the heady aroma and exquisite taste are its most endearing qualities.

Basmati rice varies a great deal in quality; like a good wine, it depends on how long the rice has been allowed to mature. Unlike other long-grain rices, basmati is matured under carefully controlled conditions for several years before being distributed for commercial use. The longer the rice is matured, the better its taste, texture and flavour. Mature rice will cook better without sticking, producing beautifully dry and fluffy grains. Young rice usually has a higher proportion of starch, which makes it prone to sticking. It is difficult to know the age of the rice as there is no indication of this on the package. Generally, the best variety of basmati rice comes from the snow-fed paddy fields at the foot of the Himalayas. If you have found a brand with which you are happy, then stay with it. Rice is also ground to make rice flour used in making sweets, dumplings, pancakes and so on; flattened to make flaked rice for delicious snacks; and puffed in very hot sand to make puffed rice for sweets.

Salt

In Indian cooking, salt is used almost as a spice and the amount required does seem higher than that used in a Western kitchen. It is generally added at the beginning or during the cooking process, not as a condiment at the end. Salt helps give the spice blend a proper balance and a well blended, rounded flavour cannot be achieved without a certain level of salt. However, bearing in mind healthy eating advice, this can be done by choosing a low sodium sea salt.

Tamarind

Tamarind concentrate or pulp is available in block form from good supermarkets as well as specialist Indian stores. It can be stored without refrigeration, unlike the tamarind juice sold in jars which, once opened, has to be kept chilled. Dried tamarind is a recent addition to the market; it is very convenient to use and keeps well.

Water or stock

Always make sure the liquid you use to cook the main ingredient of the recipe is warm before adding it. Adding cold water or stock to your carefully blended spices will impair their flavours.

Speciality spices and herbs

The following ingredients are not yet commonly available in supermarkets, however they do lend a special magic to Indian dishes and are worth seeking out in specialist Asian stores.

Aniseed
Also known as ajowain or carum, is native to India and looks like celery seed. It is used in fish dishes and deep fried food as it aids digestion.

Asafoetida (or hing)
This is a powerful ingredient used in very small quantities in pulse and vegetable dishes. You can either buy a small block and grate it with the fine side of a cheese grater as and when required, or buy a small quantity of the powder.

Curry leaves
These are sold fresh or dried in Indian shops, some specialist shops and occasionally in supermarkets. They are powerful and assertive in flavour. The fresh ones can be frozen and used as required; the dried variety will keep well in an airtight jar for several weeks.

Dried fenugreek leaves
These are native to the Mediterranean region and used freely in north Indian cooking for their aromatic qualities. You can buy them from Indian stores and they will keep well for several months.

Fenugreek seeds (methi dana)
The tiny, cream coloured seeds have a powerful taste. Only minute quantities are used and they keep well for several months.

Onion seeds
Sometimes called kalonji, these are tiny black seeds. They will keep well for months if stored in an airtight jar.

Shahi jeera
This is a rare variety of cumin also known as black cumin seeds (kala jeera) or royal cumin. They are more expensive than the common cumin seeds but have a delicate and distinctive flavour that makes them a worthwhile purchase.

White poppy seeds (khas khas)
They have a nutty taste and are used to thicken sauces. The black variety, generally used in English-speaking countries for baking, is not used in Indian cooking.

Using spices

Spices are the heart and soul of Indian cooking. Knowing how to use the spices is the key that unlocks the secrets of the alluring aromas and magical flavours of classic Indian cuisine. Indian cooking uses a varied range of spices and combines several of them in one dish to achieve the desired taste. The final result is a subtle blend of flavours without any one spice dominating.

It may sound like a difficult task, but all you need is a little patience and care in the beginning to understand how the spices work. After a while, when you start to recognise the different smells, colours and textures of the spices, you will automatically know what to do. Follow strictly the guidelines below about storing and using spices correctly. Make sure you get these two simple procedures right and your Indian dishes will turn out well every time. It is as simple as that!

Whole spices add their own distinctive bouquet and flavour to a dish. Unlike ground spices, which integrate totally into the sauce and cannot be identified later, whole spices can be removed after cooking if desired. They are usually added at the beginning of the cooking process to perfume the oil; sometimes they are added at the end to aromatise the food. Once they have released their flavours into the dish, their function is complete and they are not eaten, but left on the side of the plate.

Spices used in this way include cinnamon sticks, cardamom pods, cloves, bay leaves, curry leaves, whole chillies and whole peppercorns. They only need a few seconds to release their full flavour, so always follow the time and temperature specified in the recipe. These are the only two factors which will ensure that the characters of the spices change just enough to release their full flavours into the dish. For instance, if the heat is too high or if you fry them for too long, they will change beyond recognition, producing an unpleasant flavour.

Choose and store your whole spices carefully. Buying smaller quantities more frequently is the secret. Whole spices have essential oils in them which produce flavours ranging from mildly aromatic to intensely fiery. If you allow the essential oil to dry up, the flavour too will disappear. Store them in airtight containers in a cool dark place and use each batch of spices within 12 months.

If you have the time and the inclination to cook only with freshly ground spices, then roast each variety of whole spice (such as cumin seeds, coriander seeds, cinnamon sticks, cardamom pods and cloves) before grinding them in a coffee mill. Roasting the whole spices will enhance their aroma and taste and will make it easier to grind them to a fine powder. Once roasted and ground, they should be kept in an airtight container and used within 6 months.

Roasting is simple and takes only a few minutes. Preheat a cast-iron pan over a medium heat and add your chosen spice. Reduce the heat to low and stir until the spice releases its aroma. This usually takes 30–60 seconds. Once you have achieved this, transfer the spices to a plate to prevent them over-heating and cool before grinding down.

Although freshly ground spices have a magical aroma and taste, the pressure of modern living limits our time in the kitchen. Ready-ground spices are the answer and can perform at their best if they are removed from their commercial packaging, lightly roasted and cooled before storing. Take care not to over-heat them; remove from the pan and cool as soon as you are able to smell the aroma. Store them in airtight jars away from direct light. Not only will their flavours be enhanced, they will enjoy a longer shelf life.

To cook spices properly, they must be fried, whole or ground, following the specific time and temperature stipulated in the recipes. A little care and patience in the beginning will give delightful results. Generally, once the raw taste of the spices is eliminated or 'cooked out', Indian dishes are left to cook and require little further attention.

The five-spice mix

Panch-phoran or five-spice mix is a unique blend from the East and North East of India. It can be found ready-made in Indian shops, however you can make it up by combining a teaspoon each of cumin seeds, fennel seeds, black mustard seeds, onion seeds (see above) and ½ teaspoon of fenugreek seeds. Simply mix them together and store in an airtight jar.

Freezing Indian food

Many Indian dishes are ideal for freezing and the flavours seem enhanced when thawed and reheated. Except for potato dishes and those made from ingredients with a high water content, such as marrow, most dishes in this book can be frozen successfully. Use the following guidelines for freezing and reheating:

1 Leave the food slightly undercooked before freezing it.

2 Cool it rapidly. The best way to do this is to tip the food into a large tray (I normally use a roasting tin) and leave it in a cool place.

3 When the food has cooled, put it into freezer containers, label and chill thoroughly in the fridge before placing it in the freezer. This will help the food keep well for up to 6 months.

4 If you want to freeze any leftovers, use the above guidelines but consume the food within 3 months.

5 Thaw frozen food slowly and thoroughly and make sure that the food is piping hot before you serve it. If you have a temperature probe, use it. Generally bugs are killed at 85°C/185°F. Thawed food will have a certain amount of water separation but, once heated, it will return to its normal consistency as the water will be absorbed by the solid ingredients.

6 When reheating dry foods such as any of the tandoori dishes and kababs, wrap them in a double thickness of foil and place in the centre of a hot oven until piping hot. It is difficult to give precise timings as oven temperatures vary considerably. It is simply a matter of checking either with a temperature probe or using your judgement. You can also use microwave ovens to heat thawed food, but always cover the food to ensure that it does not dry out.

Cooking utensils

There are some cooking utensils that are ideal for each particular technique, although for most you can use equipment that you will probably already have in your kitchen. Each chapter gives some indication of what is ideal to use.

For preparing baghar dishes, normal utensils are suitable for this style of cooking, although there are special Indian-made cast-iron pans that are available in specialist shops.

Bhuna recipes require more work as food is stir-fried and so heavy pans are more ideal to ensure that the heat is evenly distributed as well as retained while cooking.

Steamed dishes, called dum, are more specialized and will need special equipment for perfect results. Heavey saucepans with tight-fitting lids, in particular, are essential.

Similarly, korma recipes will require heavy pans with lids to ensure that the food is well-braised and then cooked slowly for a long period of time until tender.

For tandoori cooking, the word does in fact originate from the tandoor, which is a barrel-shaped clay oven. It is ideal to use if you have one but since the techniques of cooking that are used vary from grilling and roasting to baking, your usual appliances will still work. They are also used for cooking kababs and so are very flexible and easy-to-use.

Another key way of cooking Indian food is with the karahi, which is a heavy cast-iron pan shaped like a wok. This is used for talana dishes which require very heavy deep frying.

Baghar
Seasoning

The secret of unlocking flavours

Baghar, or tadka (also known as tarka), is a simple and effective technique used to perfume the oil or ghee (Indian clarified butter) which is folded into a finished dish to intensify its flavour. The heady aroma of the spices when fried in hot oil seems to have a magical power to lure anyone remotely interested in cooking into the kitchen.

The technique is used mainly for flavouring vegetables, lentils and salads, and sometimes for meat and fish dishes. The combination of spices varies from region to region, as does the cooking medium. Oil is most commonly used but ghee will add a richer flavour. The fat is heated to a fairly high temperature and whole spices such as cumin seeds, dried red chillies, black pepper, cloves, cardamom, cinnamon and so on are added to the oil. Sometimes a combination of whole and ground spices is used for a tadka. The whole spices take 10–15 seconds to release their flavour, at which point the heat should be turned off and the ground spices stirred into the oil. The entire contents of the pan is then folded into the finished dish. A baghar or tadka of onions, ginger, garlic and other flavourings is also used in many dishes.

Normal cooking utensils are adequate for this technique. It is the size of the pan that is most important and a small saucepan (the size of a milk pan or smaller) is ideal. In India specially made miniature pans, shaped like a wok, are used for seasoning. These are usually made of cast–iron or heavy aluminium and steel.

I prefer to use a steel ladle as it seems to intensify the flavours. I normally have all my seasoning ingredients ready before heating the oil in the ladle, which I hold over the heat source with one hand. As soon as the oil is hot, throw in the spices. In a few seconds they will release the most amazing perfume. You simply immerse the ladle into the dish you want to season and hold it for a few seconds until it stops sizzling. The result will be a spectacular taste and aroma.

Dhal Panch-phoron
Red lentils with five-spice seasoning

There is something inviting about the earthy smell of gently simmering lentils. They have a good, wholesome taste of their own and can be adapted to suit winter or summer eating equally well, depending on what you add to them. This is one of my favourite lentil dishes; simple, but deliciously flavoured with five-spice mix. I like to use ghee for seasoning simple lentil dishes because a magical transformation takes place in the process, giving the dish the most incredible flavour. As a child I remember being lured into the kitchen by the glorious aroma of fried five-spice mix and chillies. My grandmother would give me one of her loving smiles as if to say 'I know what attracted you into the kitchen!' Over a period of time, I learnt to recognise the dish by this aroma alone and you, too will find this. Train your nose to distinguish between the variations in the aroma and its relationship to the final taste of the dish. It's easy!

Serves 4

225 g/8 oz/1 cup red split lentils

½ tsp ground turmeric

1 tsp salt, or to taste

2 tbsp ghee

½ tsp five-spice mix

3–4 small dried red chillies

Wash the lentils thoroughly and drain. Put them in a saucepan with the turmeric and add 1 litre/1½ pints/4½ cups of water. Bring to the boil and remove the froth with a slotted spoon. Boil for 3–5 minutes, then reduce the heat to low and stir in the salt. Cover the pan and simmer for about 25–30 minutes, stirring the lentils once or twice during cooking.

Heat the ghee in a steel ladle or a very small saucepan over a medium heat until almost smoking. Turn the heat off and throw in the five-spice mix followed by the chillies. Allow the chillies to blacken a little, then tilt the uncovered pan of lentils slightly and immerse the ladle in it. When it stops sizzling, swirl the ladle around so that the spices are well distributed in the lentils, then remove the ladle. Keep the pan covered until you are ready to serve. The small chillies are not meant to be eaten unless you are a chilli freak!

My Secrets

Lentils often have tiny white, or sometimes black, stones. Scan the lentils well, then wash them thoroughly before cooking.

The five-spice mix lends a nutty flavour to the dish whose balance of flavours is typical of the north-eastern region of India.

One of the tricks of cooking spices is to always heat them in hot oil which is not hot enough to make them burn and turn bitter.

Masoor Mussallam

Spiced whole red lentils

Serves 4

225 g/8 oz/1 cup whole red lentils or whole green lentils

3 tbsp ghee or unsalted butter

1 medium onion, finely chopped

2.5 cm/1 in cube root ginger, finely grated or 2 tsp ginger purée

½–1 tsp chilli powder

1 tsp ground turmeric

125 g/4 oz/½ cup thick set plain yogurt

1 tsp salt, or to taste

2 small, ripe tomatoes, skinned and chopped

1–2 green chillies, deseeded and chopped

1 tsp cumin seeds

2–3 large cloves garlic, crushed or 1½ tsp garlic purée

½ tsp garam masala

The lentils used in this recipe are the whole red ones (whole masoor dhal) with the skin intact. When the skin is removed and the lentils are split, they are known as masoor dhal, or red split lentils, and are the most common type sold in the West. Whole lentils have a very earthy and inviting taste and aroma and are a great source of fibre. They are sold by Indian grocers and some health food shops. If you cannot get whole red lentils, use the whole green lentils sold in supermarkets.

Wash the lentils in several changes of water until the water runs clear and leave to drain.

In a heavy saucepan, melt 2 tablespoons of the ghee or butter over a low heat and add the onion and ginger. Increase the heat to medium and fry for 6–8 minutes until the onion begins to brown. Stir in the chilli powder and turmeric followed by the lentils. Stir-fry the lentils for 3–4 minutes.

Pour in 600 ml/1 pint/2½ cups hot water. Bring the mixture to the boil, then reduce the heat to low. Cover the pan and simmer for about 30–35 minutes.

In a small bowl, whisk the yogurt and add it to the lentils along with the salt. Stir in the chopped tomatoes and reduce the heat to the lowest setting. Leave the lentils gently simmering while you prepare the seasoning.

In a steel ladle, melt the remaining ghee or butter over a medium heat and add the chillies, cumin and garlic. Let the garlic brown slightly, then stir in the garam masala and cook for 10–15 seconds. Immerse the ladle in the pot of lentils and hold until it stops sizzling. Remove the ladle and keep the pot of lentils covered until you are ready to dish up. Serve with Sada Pulao (Plain pilau rice), see page 119, and a kabab or a tandoori dish.

My Secrets

Make sure that the heat is kept low while lentils cook as they will not soften at high temperatures.

Wait till the dish is brought to the table before uncovering it and watch the magical transformation of mood when the exquisite aroma of the seasoning ingredients is released!

Masoor Masala

Spiced red lentils

Humble red lentils are given very special treatment here. Their wholesome taste is superb combined with these flavourings and their pale colour lends a confetti-like effect to the presentation. To me, lentils are reminiscent of festive occasions. Not only are they cooked in many different and delicious ways, skilful housewives create patterns on the floor using lentils of different colours. Red lentils always feature prominently in these patterns.

Wash the lentils in several changes of water and leave to drain.

In a heavy saucepan (preferably with a non-stick surface), heat 2 tablespoons of the oil over a medium heat. When hot but not smoking, throw in the mustard seeds and as soon as they start to pop, add the cumin. Let them sizzle and pop for 15–20 seconds, then add the lentils and stir-fry for 2–3 minutes. Add the ground cumin, turmeric and salt and stir-fry for a further 2–3 minutes.

Pour in 1 litre/1½ pints/4 cups lukewarm water. Bring the mixture to the boil, reduce the heat to low and cook uncovered for 5–6 minutes. Then cover the pan and cook for 30 minutes or until the lentils have become tender.

Meanwhile, during the last 10 minutes of the cooking time, prepare the seasoning. Heat the remaining 2 tablespoons of oil in a sauté pan over a medium heat. Add the shallots and stir-fry for 3–4 minutes, reduce the heat to low, then add the ginger, garlic and chillies and stir-fry for 2 minutes. Mix in the tomatoes and stir-fry for 1 minute before adding the coriander (cilantro).

Tip the entire contents of the sauté pan into the lentils, stir and remove from the heat. Serve with boiled basmati rice accompanied by kababs or any tandoori dishes. For a vegetarian meal, serve with rice, raita and a dry-spiced vegetable dish.

Serves 4

225 g/8 oz/1 cup red split lentils (masoor dhal)

4 tbsp sunflower or vegetable oil

½ tsp black mustard seeds

½ tsp cumin seeds

1½ tsp ground cumin

1 tsp ground turmeric

1 tsp salt, or to taste

6 shallots, finely chopped

1 cm/½ in cube root ginger, finely grated

2 cloves garlic, crushed

1–3 green chillies, deseeded and finely chopped

2 ripe tomatoes, skinned and chopped

2 tbsp coriander (cilantro) leaves, finely chopped

My Secrets

For a more interesting and intensified flavour, use equal quantities of red lentils and yellow split lentils (moong dhal).

Frying the ginger, garlic and chillies over a low heat will intensify their flavours giving a far superior taste to the dish.

Baigan aur Kabuli Channa ki Kari

Aubergine (eggplant) and chickpea (garbanzo) curry

Serves 4

1 large aubergine (eggplant), about 285 g/ 10 oz/1¼ cups

1 tbsp coriander seeds

2–6 dried red chillies, broken

4 tbsp sunflower or soya oil

½ tsp ground turmeric

1 tsp salt, or to taste

1 x 400 g/14 oz can chickpeas (garbanzos), drained and rinsed

4 tbsp coconut milk powder or creamed coconut, grated, or purée

1 tbsp lime juice

6 large cloves garlic, crushed

I simply adore the beautiful, shiny purple skin and the smooth, velvety texture of aubergine (eggplant). Although there are many different types, it is the large purple variety, along with the small white ones, that I have grown up eating. They were grown in our back garden every year and I enjoyed plucking them for my mother. The nutty taste of chickpeas (garbanzos) complements the flavour and texture of the aubergine (eggplant) perfectly.

Cut the aubergine (eggplant) into 5 cm/2 in cubes and soak them in salted water for 15–20 minutes. Rinse well and drain.

In a coffee or spice mill, finely grind the coriander and chillies and set aside.

Heat 3 tablespoons of the oil in a medium saucepan over a low heat. Add the ground coriander and chilli mixture and fry gently for 15–20 seconds. Add the drained aubergine (eggplant) and turmeric. Increase the heat to medium and stir-fry for 25–30 seconds. Add the salt and chickpeas (garbanzos).

Dissolve the coconut milk powder or creamed coconut in 300 ml/ ½ pint/1¼ cups of hot water and add it to the pan. Reduce the heat to low, cover and cook for 10–12 minutes or until the aubergine (eggplant) is tender. Stir in the lime juice and remove from the heat. Keep the pan covered while you prepare the baghar.

Using a steel ladle, heat the remaining 1 tablespoon of oil over a medium heat and add the garlic. Reduce the heat to low and let the garlic sizzle until lightly browned. Immerse the ladle into the curry and hold until it stops sizzling. Remove the ladle, stir the curry gently to mix the seasoning and keep the pan covered until you are ready to serve.

My Secrets

Chickpeas (garbanzos) grow extensively in India. The pea pods are threshed and sun-dried before being used. I have used canned chickpeas (garbanzos), but if you want to use dried ones, you will need to soak them overnight and cook them until they are tender before starting this dish.

If you are using creamed coconut, do not worry if it is not completely dissolved before adding it to the pan.

Lasoon aur Mirchiwali Subzi

Vegetables with garlic and chillies

This is a fabulous mixture of root vegetables stir-fried in sunflower oil that has been flavoured with a few whole spices, garlic and chillies. It makes a wonderful accompaniment to any meat or poultry dish.

Peel the vegetables and cut them like french fries, but half their length, about 2.5 cm/1 in. Soak them in salted water for 15–20 minutes, then rinse thoroughly. Drain and dry with a clean cloth.

Heat the oil in a non-stick sauté pan over a low heat. When hot but not smoking, throw in the mustard seeds. As they begin to crackle, add the cumin, then the fenugreek and garlic together. Fry gently until the garlic begins to brown a little.

Stir in the turmeric and chilli powder, then the vegetables and salt. Increase the heat to medium and stir-fry the vegetables for 4–5 minutes. Reduce the heat slightly, cover the pan and cook, stirring regularly, for 8–10 minutes or until the vegetables are tender but firm and have brown patches.

Add the coriander (cilantro) leaves and stir-fry for 1 minute, then remove from the heat and serve. This dish is not 'seasoned' as with the other dishes in this chapter.

Serves 4

2 potatoes, about 225 g/ 8 oz/1 cup

2 parsnips, about 225 g/ 8 oz/1 cup

2 carrots, about 225 g/8 oz/ 1 cup

4 tbsp sunflower oil

½ tsp black mustard seeds

½ tsp cumin seeds

8–10 fenugreek seeds

4–5 large cloves garlic, crushed

½ tsp ground turmeric

½–1 tsp chilli powder

1 tsp salt

2 tbsp coriander (cilantro) leaves, chopped

My Secrets

The seasoning takes place in oil and at the beginning of the recipe in this dish.

When heating the oil, watch it carefully so that it is at the right temperature. Wait until ripples appear at the bottom of the pan and as soon as they begin to become faint, throw in the seeds. The intense, nutty flavour of the mustard seeds will be fully released, which is important.

Adrak aur Tamatar ke Aloo

Potatoes with ginger and chillies

Serves 4

4 tbsp sunflower or soya oil

5 cm/2 in cube root ginger, grated

1–3 green chillies, cut into strips

½ tsp ground turmeric

700 g/1½ lb boiled potatoes, peeled and cut into bite-size pieces

1 tsp salt, or to taste

2 ripe tomatoes, skinned and chopped

1 tbsp fresh curry leaves

When I visited South India recently, this simple potato dish became my firm favourite. The flavour is intensified with fresh curry leaves and root ginger. The appearance too is striking, with a pale turmeric-yellow background showing off the pieces of tomatoes, curry leaves and green chillies. Yum, yum!

In a non-stick sauté pan, heat the oil over a low heat and add the ginger and chillies. Fry them gently for 2 minutes. Stir in the turmeric and cook for 30 seconds. Add the potatoes and salt and cook until the potatoes are heated through, stirring frequently.

Add the tomatoes and curry leaves and cook for 2–3 minutes. Remove the pan from the heat and serve with Palak Puri (Deep-fried puffed bread with spinach), see page 138, accompanied by Shami Kabab (Spiced minced lamb patties), see page 100, or Peshawari Kabab (Peshawar-style skewered lamb), see page 102, if liked.

My Secrets

As I originate from north India, where coriander (cilantro) and mint leaves are most commonly used, I have come to adore the fresh, lingering smell of curry leaves used by my mother-in-law in southern India. When she fried these strong-smelling leaves in coconut oil, the air filled with a kind of magic that is unforgettable! If you cannot get them, use plenty of fresh coriander – though the flavour will not be the same, it is just as delicious.

Remember you can deseed the green chillies for a milder taste.

Methi Subzi

Vegetables with fenugreek

A colourful combination of vegetables, this makes a superb accompaniment to a meat, fish or poultry dish. For a vegetarian meal, combine it with a protein-rich dish such as Dhal Panch-phoron (Red lentils with five-spice seasoning), see page 19, or Paneer Pasanda (Marinated pan-fried strips of Indian cheese), see page 93.

In a saucepan, bring 450 ml/¾ pint/2 cups of water to the boil and add the beans (haricots verts) and carrots. Bring back to the boil, reduce the heat to medium and cook, covered, for 5 minutes. Add the cauliflower, coconut milk and salt then cover the pan and cook for 5 minutes.

Meanwhile, in a small pan or a steel ladle, heat ½ tablespoon of the oil over a low heat and add the fenugreek and chillies. Fry gently until they are just a shade darker but not deep brown. Remove from the heat and cool. Using a pestle and mortar, crush the fenugreek and chillies into the oil to make a paste. Stir the paste into the vegetable mixture then remove the vegetables from the heat and keep the pan covered.

Heat the remaining 2½ tablespoons of oil in a small saucepan or sauté pan over a medium heat. When hot but not smoking, add the mustard seeds. As soon as they begin to pop, add the onion and fry for 9–10 minutes or until light brown, stirring regularly. Add the turmeric, stir then add to the vegetables.

Place the pan of vegetables back over a medium heat and let it simmer for 2–3 minutes. Stir in the tamarind or lime juice, remove from the heat and serve.

Serves 4

90 g/3 oz/½ cup whole green beans (haricots verts), cut into 2.5 cm/1 in pieces

90 g/3 oz/½ cup carrots, peeled and cut into bite-size pieces

350 g/12 oz/1½ cups cauliflower florets, cut into 1 cm/½ in pieces

175 ml/6 fl oz/¾ cup canned coconut milk

1 tsp salt, or to taste

3 tbsp sunflower or soya oil

½ tsp fenugreek seeds

1–4 dried red chillies, chopped

½ tsp black mustard seeds

1 medium onion, finely chopped

½ tsp ground turmeric

1½ tbsp tamarind juice or 1 tbsp lime juice

My Secret

It is such a shame to waste any of the flavoured oil, so I usually crush the spices directly in the pan instead of transferring them to a mortar. It is easy to crush them with the back of a wooden spoon or a wooden pestle.

Baghare Tamatar

Tomatoes with hot oil seasoning

Serves 4–5

700 g/1½ lb/3 cups medium tomatoes, skinned

2 tbsp sunflower or vegetable oil

½ tsp cumin seeds

½ tsp onion seeds (kalonji)

2.5 cm/1 in cube root ginger, finely grated

3–4 cloves garlic, crushed

2 green chillies, finely chopped

½ tsp ground turmeric

¼–½ tsp black pepper, coarsely crushed

2 tbsp coriander (cilantro) leaves and stalks, finely chopped

1 tbsp fresh curry leaves, or 8–10 dried

1 tsp salt, or to taste

½ tsp sugar

4 tbsp creamed coconut, grated

The distinctive flavour of this simple but deliciously aromatic dish comes from curry leaves. Fresh or dried curry leaves are sold in all Indian shops. The dried ones should be stored in airtight jars and the fresh ones can be frozen and used as and when required straight from the freezer. Deseed the green chillies if you prefer.

Cut the tomatoes in half and cut each half into quarters.

In a medium saucepan, heat the oil over a medium-low heat and add the cumin and onion seeds. Fry them for 15–20 seconds, then add the ginger, garlic and chillies and fry gently for 2 minutes until browned. Add the turmeric and pepper, stir-fry for 30 seconds, then add the tomatoes and all the remaining ingredients and mix well.

Pour in 150 ml/5 fl oz/⅔ cup of lukewarm water. Bring to the boil, reduce the heat to low, cover and simmer for 10 minutes.

Remove the lid and cook, uncovered, for 5–6 minutes or until the mixture has thickened. Serve with boiled basmati rice, Noor Mahal Biryani (Rice steamed with aromatic lamb), see page 62, or Jeera Chawal (Cumin flavoured rice), see page 120, accompanied by any kabab or tandoori dish.

My Secret

For this recipe, whenever possible, I like to follow my sister's secret method for peeling tomatoes. She gives them a smoky flavour by placing them under a preheated grill or broiler until the skin is split and charred. The skin comes away quite easily once they start to split.

Tamatar ki Rasewali Machchi

Fish in aromatic tomato sauce

This is the kind of fish curry I grew up eating. In the North-Eastern part of India, fish is a standard item on the menu and those found in local waters are firm, dense and delicious. My mother would carefully cover the seasoned dish with a tight fitting lid to keep all the aroma and flavour intact while taking it to the table.

Cut each fish steak into 3–4 thick slices, sprinkle with ½ teaspoon of the salt and set aside.

In a blender, purée the ginger, garlic and chillies, adding a little water if necessary to make a paste; alternatively, crush them to a fine paste using a pestle and mortar.

In a frying pan, heat 3 tablespoons of the oil over a medium heat and add the onion. Fry, stirring frequently, until the onion is soft and slightly browned. Add the puréed ingredients and continue cooking for 30–40 seconds. Add the ground aniseed and turmeric and stir-fry for 1 minute.

Mix in the sieved tomatoes and the remaining ½ teaspoon of salt and cook for 2–3 minutes. Stir in 150 ml/5 fl oz/⅔ cup of lukewarm water and let the sauce simmer gently for a minute or so. Add the fish, cover the pan, reduce the heat to low and cook for 10–12 minutes.

In a steel ladle, heat the remaining tablespoon of oil over a medium heat. When hot, switch off the stove and add the black mustard, onion and fenugreek seeds. Let them sizzle for 15–20 seconds then carefully immerse the ladle in the tomato sauce. Remove the ladle and carefully stir the flavoured oil into the sauce. Keep the pan covered until you are ready to serve, accompanied by boiled basmati rice garnished with the coriander leaves.

Serves 4

4 tuna steaks, about 700 g/1½ lb

1 tsp salt, or to taste

2.5 cm/1 in cube root ginger, roughly chopped

4 large cloves garlic, roughly chopped

2–4 green chillies, deseeded and roughly chopped

4 tbsp sunflower or soya oil

1 large onion, finely chopped

1 tsp ground aniseed

1 tsp ground turmeric

200 ml/7 fl oz/1 cup chopped canned tomatoes, sieved

½ tsp black mustard seeds

½ tsp onion seeds

8–10 fenugreek seeds

2 tbsp coriander (cilantro) leaves, chopped

My Secrets

My choice here is tuna steaks, but you could use any firm fish, including frozen varieties. If you are using frozen fish, thaw completely and pat dry with absorbent paper first.

It saves time and effort if you use passata (Italian sieved tomato) instead of canned tomatoes which you have to sieve yourself.

Jinghewale Dhal

Prawns (shrimp) with lentils

Serves 4

175 g/6 oz/¾ cup channa dhal, washed and soaked for 1–2 hours

½ tsp ground turmeric

½ tsp crushed dried chillies

1 medium tomato

3 tbsp sunflower or vegetable oil

5 cm/2 in stick cinnamon

6 green cardamom pods, bruised

4 cloves

2 bay leaves, crumpled

1–3 green chillies, deseeded and finely chopped

2.5 cm/1 in cube root ginger, finely grated

2 tsp ground coriander

1 tsp ground cumin

400 g/14 oz/1½ cups cooked and peeled king prawns (shrimp), thawed and drained if necessary

1 tsp salt, or to taste

3 tbsp coriander (cilantro) leaves and stalks, finely chopped

2 tbsp lemon juice

This is a superb combination of channa dhal (split Bengal gram) and succulent king prawns (shrimp). Instead of channa dhal, you can use yellow split peas, though the latter does not have the same wonderful nutty flavour.

Drain the dhal and place in a saucepan with 600 ml/1 pint/2½ cups water. Bring to the boil and add the turmeric and chillies. Reduce the heat to low, partially cover the pan and cook for 25–30 minutes or until the dahl is tender. Using the back of a spoon, mash some of the dahl by pressing against the side of the pan.

Meanwhile, place the tomato in a bowl and cover with boiling water. Leave for 1 minute, then plunge the tomato into cold water. Peel away the skin, scoop out and discard the seeds and chop the flesh roughly.

In a frying pan, heat the oil over low heat and add the cinnamon, cardamom, cloves and bay leaves. Let them sizzle for 20–25 seconds. Add the chillies and ginger and fry gently for 2–3 minutes. Add the coriander and cumin and cook for 1 minute before adding the prawns (shrimp), tomato and salt. Increase the heat to medium and cook for 3–4 minutes.

Pour the prawn (shrimp) mixture into the dhal. Add the coriander (cilantro) and lemon juice and cook for 2–3 minutes. Remove from the heat and serve with boiled basmati rice and a raita.

My Secrets

My grandmother cooked beautiful, succulent river prawns (shrimp) to perfection. She told me that the secret of keeping them succulent is to take them off the heat as soon as they begin to curl up. Prolonged cooking makes them chewy.

The dhal are mashed a little to thicken the sauce. Instead of pressing them against the side of the pan, you can use a hand blender if you prefer, just for a few seconds.

Baghare Aloo Gosht

Meat and potato curry with hot oil seasoning

This is a simple, home-style dish which was my mother's speciality. She used mutton, but it is equally delicious with lean beef or pork. I have used pork leg steaks, but you could also use braising steak.

Heat 4 tablespoons of oil over a medium heat, then fry the onion for 5–6 minutes until soft but not brown.

Add the meat, ginger, garlic, turmeric, fennel, coriander and the chilli powder.

Stir-fry over a medium-high heat for 4–5 minutes or until the meat changes colour.

Add the stock and vinegar, bring the mixture to the boil, then reduce the heat and cover the pan. Simmer gently for 40–45 minutes.

Add the potatoes and salt. Stir, cover and simmer for a further 20–25 minutes or until the meat and potatoes are tender.

In a small pan or steel ladle, heat the remaining oil over a low heat and add the cinnamon, cloves, fennel seeds and bay leaves. Let them sizzle for 15–20 seconds, then immerse the ladle into the saucepan containing the meat and potatoes. Hold it for a few seconds then remove the ladle Stir the meat curry to distribute the seasoning well. Cover and set aside until required.

Serve with bread.

My Secrets

Sometimes, if I am in the mood for a richer taste, I add about 50 ml/ 2fl oz/¼ cup single (thin) cream before adding the seasoning. You could also try créme fraîche or fromage frais.

Fennel seeds can be ground in a coffee or spice mill. Grind only a small quantity at a time as they will lose flavour if stored for a long time. Generally, they will stay fresh for 2–3 weeks.

Serves 4–5

5 tbsp sunflower oil

1 large onion, finely chopped

700 g/1½ lb/3¾ cups trimmed pork leg steaks, cut into 2.5 cm/1 in cubes

2.5 cm/1 in cube root ginger, finely grated

4–5 large cloves garlic, crushed

1 tsp ground turmeric

1½ tsp ground fennel

1½ tsp ground coriander

1 tsp chilli powder

300 ml/½ pint/1¼ cup vegetable stock or warm water

3 tbsp white wine vinegar

240 g/8 oz/1½ cups potatoes, peeled and cut into bite-sized pieces

1 tsp salt, or to taste

2.5 cm/1 in piece cinnamon stick

4 cloves

½ tsp fennel seeds

2 bay leaves

Bhuna

Stir-frying

The art of stir-frying

I remember the winter nights at home, with cold Himalayan breezes, when my mother produced the most warming meals consisting of dry bhuna (or bhoona) dishes and kitchdi, a beautifully moist rice and lentil dish perfumed with winter spices.

The bhuna method involves frying the spices over a high heat while adding small amounts of water at regular intervals to prevent them burning. During this process, the spices will stick very slightly to the sides and bottom of the pan. Adding water reduces the temperature, enabling the cook to scrape up the sticking spices and mix them with the remainder in the pan. It is this technique, of scraping, stirring and mixing the spices without letting them burn, that unlocks the enticing flavours of a bhuna dish.

Heavy cooking utensils are ideal for this method because they will distribute and retain heat evenly allowing the food to cook to perfection. Sometimes, after the spices are fried off, the food is cooked by gentle sweating. Halfway through, salt is added to help the food release its natural juices and keep the dish moist. Small quantities of water may also be added to help cook the food. The dish is then finished with a short burst of stir-frying over a fairly high heat. Another way of cooking a bhuna dish is to marinate the meat or poultry and fry it over a high heat, adding a little water from time to time, until cooked.

Bhuna dishes are normally served with bread, but they are equally delicious with plain boiled basmati rice if accompanied by a simple lentil dish as well.

Aubergine and Chickpea Curry (page 22)

Vegetables with Garlic and Chillies (page 23) and Dry Fruit and Nuts in Spiced Yogurt (page 144)

Okra with Onions (page 33) and Stir-fried Meatballs (page 42)

Baby Corn Fritters (page 107) and Rice Steamed with Aromatic Lamb (page 62)

Slow-cooked Lamb with Turnips (page 60)

Bhindi-Piaz

Okra with onions

Okra stir-fried with onions and spices makes a superb accompaniment to any meat, poultry or fish dish. It is quick and easy to cook and has a fresh, colourful appearance.

Scrub the okra gently and wash them thoroughly. Remove the hard head and trim off the tail.

Cut them diagonally into 2–3 large pieces, depending on their size; if they are really tender, simply top and tail them and leave them whole.

Heat the oil in a heavy non-stick sauté or frying pan over a medium heat. Throw in the black mustard seeds and, as soon as they start popping, add the cumin seeds. Add the okra, onion, bell pepper, spices and salt. Increase the heat slightly and stir-fry for 6–7 minutes until the vegetables have browned a little.

Put the besan or wholemeal flour into a sieve and sprinkle it evenly over the vegetables. Reduce the heat to low and cook for 1–2 minutes, stirring constantly. Remove from the heat and serve.

Serves 4

500 g/1 lb okra (ladies' fingers or bhindi)

5 tbsp sunflower or soya oil

½ tsp black mustard seeds

½ tsp cumin seeds

1 large onion, halved and thickly sliced

1 red bell pepper, cut into 5 cm/2 in strips

1 tsp ground coriander

1 tsp ground cumin

½–1 tsp chilli powder

1 tsp salt, or to taste

2 tbsp besan (gram flour), or 1 tbsp wholemeal flour

My Secrets
Keep the temperature steady throughout. The okra needs to be browned quickly. A lower heat will give soggy or sticky okra.

If the okra you are using is tender, top and tail them but leave them whole.

Masaledar Ghia

Spiced marrow

Serves 4–6

4 tbsp sunflower or soya oil

1 tsp five-spice mix

1 large onion, very finely chopped

2 cloves garlic, crushed

1 cm/½ in cube root ginger, finely grated

225 g/8 oz/1 cup chopped canned tomatoes in tomato juice

½ tsp ground turmeric

½–1 tsp chilli powder

1 tsp ground coriander

½ tsp ground cumin

125 ml/4 fl oz/½ cup lukewarm water

700 g/1½ lb tender marrow or courgettes (zucchini), cut into bite-size pieces

1 tsp salt, or to taste

Marrow plants with their soft tender fruit, beautiful golden flowers with a faint green tinge and large, emerald leaves always made a pretty picture in my mother's sunny orchard back in India. She used the flowers for spicy fritters which were to die for! For my lightly spiced recipe here, you can use tender marrow or courgettes (zucchini).

In a heavy pan, heat the oil over a medium heat, add the five-spice mix and cook for 15–20 seconds. Add the onion and fry for 9–10 minutes or until light brown, stirring frequently.

Add the garlic and ginger and cook for 1 minute, then add the tomatoes and stir-fry for 1–2 minutes. Reduce the heat to low, cover the pan and cook for 4–5 minutes.

Add the turmeric and chilli powder and cook for 1 minute. Then add the coriander and cumin, increase the heat to medium-high and stir-fry for 2–3 minutes. Add one-third of the lukewarm water and continue to stir-fry for 2–3 minutes. Repeat this process twice with the remaining water.

Add the marrow or courgettes (zucchini) and salt, mixing well. Reduce the heat to low, cover the pan and cook, stirring occasionally, until the vegetables are tender but still firm, about 10–12 minutes. Serve as an accompaniment to any meat, poultry or fish dish.

My Secrets

The method of preparing the spices imparts a delicious toasted aroma into the dish.

The trick here is to almost let the spices stick to the pan and then to add more water to stop it burning.

Shalgam ka Bharta

Spiced turnip purée

Turnips are very low in calories and they provide plenty of dietary fibre. I eat them without feeling guilty even though some fat is added here during cooking!

Preheat the oven to 200°C/400°F/Gas 6. Peel the turnips and cut them into 2.5 cm/1 in cubes. Put them in a roasting tin and add 1 tablespoon of the oil, rubbing it well into the turnips with your fingertips. Roast them just above the centre of the oven for 20 minutes or until tender and brown. Remove from the oven and cool for a few minutes, then mash them roughly using a fork or the pulse action of a food processor.

In a heavy sauté or frying pan, heat the remaining 3 tablespoons of oil over a medium heat and add the cumin and onion seeds. Let them sizzle for 15–20 seconds, then add the onion, ginger and chillies and fry for 6–7 minutes, stirring frequently. Add the turmeric and fennel and stir-fry for 1 minute.

Add 2–3 tablespoons of water to the pan and stir-fry until the water evaporates. Repeat this process once more, then add the mashed turnips and salt and stir-fry for 4–5 minutes, reducing the heat slightly if necessary.

Stir in the coriander (cilantro) leaves and remove from the heat. Serve as a side dish with any bhuna, baghar or dum dishes.

Serves 4

700 g/1½ lb turnips

4 tbsp sunflower or vegetable oil

½ tsp cumin seeds

½ tsp onion seeds

1 medium onion, finely chopped

2.5 cm/1 in cube root ginger, finely grated

1–2 green chillies, deseeded and finely chopped

½ tsp ground turmeric

½ tsp ground fennel

½ tsp salt, or to taste

2–3 tbsp coriander (cilantro) leaves and stalks, finely chopped

My Secrets

If the turnips are really fresh, do not peel them. To determine their freshness, look at the tops – they should be bright green.

To enhance the final flavour of this dish, use fennel seeds rather than pre-ground fennel. Crush the seeds lightly just before adding to the pan.

Aloo Posto

Potatoes with poppy seeds

Serves 4

700 g/1½ lb potatoes

2 tbsp white poppy seeds

4 tbsp sunflower or soya oil

1 tsp five-spice mix

4–5 large cloves garlic, crushed

1–2 green chillies, deseeded and finely chopped

½ tsp ground turmeric

1 tsp salt, or to taste

A masterpiece from Bengal and the North Eastern region, potatoes with poppy seeds is simple, quick and very inviting.

Peel the potatoes and cut them into 1 cm/½ in cubes. In a bowl of water, soak them for 15 minutes to remove the starch, then drain and dry thoroughly with a cloth.

Preheat a small, heavy skillet or small pan over a medium heat. When hot, reduce the heat to low, add the poppy seeds and dry-roast the seeds, stirring constantly, for about 1 minute or until they are just a shade darker, but not dark brown. Remove the seeds from the pan, leave them to cool, then grind them using a spice or coffee mill, or a pestle and mortar.

In a heavy non-stick sauté pan or frying pan, heat 2 tablespoons of the oil over a medium-high heat and add the potatoes. Fry them, stirring frequently, for 5–8 minutes or until lightly browned. Remove with a slotted spoon and drain on absorbent paper.

Add the remaining 2 tablespoons of oil to the pan and reduce the heat to low. Add the five-spice mix and stir-fry for 30 seconds, then add the garlic and chillies and continue to fry gently until garlic has turned light brown. Stir in the fried potatoes, turmeric and salt, mix well, then add 125 ml/4 fl oz/½ cup of lukewarm water and reduce the heat to low. Cover the pan and cook gently for 8–10 minutes or until the potatoes are tender but still firm.

Add the ground poppy seeds to the potato mixture. Increase the heat slightly and stir-fry until the potatoes have absorbed any excess liquid and are fully coated with the poppy seeds. Remove from the heat and serve with Palak Puri (Deep-fried puffed bread with spinach), see page 130, accompanied by a meat or vegetable curry, if wished.

My Secrets

Potatoes lose flavour and nutrition if stored for too long. Always store them in a cool, dark place. If one or two green patches appear, slice them off thickly and discard; use these potatoes only for roasting or deep-frying.

This is a dry dish with a toasted nutty flavour. The poppy seeds are used to thicken the sauce as flour is not used as a thickening agent in Indian cooking. Make sure you do not brown them as this will dry out the natural oil and flavour of the recipe.

Bhuna hua Moong Dhal

Fried split yellow lentils

*Moong dhal is ideal for bhuna dishes as it cooks very quickly.
Although it may require a trip to an Indian store to purchase them, it is
well worth it because of the time you will save in cooking them.*

Pick over the lentils then wash and drain them thoroughly.

Heat the oil in a large, heavy non-stick pan and add the onion. Fry,
stirring frequently, for 8–10 minutes or until well browned, reducing
the heat slightly towards the last 3–4 minutes of cooking. Swich off
the heat. Use a slotted spoon to lift the onion and press down on it
with another spoon to squeeze the excess oil back into the pan.
Drain the fried onion on absorbent kitchen paper.

In the same pan, sauté the cinnamon, cardamom, bay leaf and
cumin seeds gently over a low heat for 30–40 seconds. Add the
lentils, increase the heat to medium and stir-fry for 4–5 minutes. Add
the turmeric and chilli powder and continue stir-frying for a further
2–3 minutes.

Mix in the salt and 125 ml/4 fl oz/½ cup of lukewarm water. Increase
the heat slightly to medium-high and stir-fry the mixture until the water
dries up. Repeat this process once more, then add 300 ml/½ pint/1¼
cups of warm water and reduce the heat to medium-low.

Reserve a little fried onion to use as a garnish and stir the rest into
the lentils. Cover the pan and cook for 12–15 minutes, until the lentils
are tender, but not mushy, and have absorbed all the water. Remove
from the heat and serve garnished with reserved fried onions and
strips of fresh green chilli.

Serves 4

225 g/8 oz/1 cup split
yellow lentils (moong dhal)

3–4 tbsp sunflower or soya
oil

1 large onion, finely sliced

5 cm/2 in stick cinnamon,
halved

4 green cardamom pods,
bruised

1 bay leaf, crumpled

½ tsp cumin seeds

1 tsp ground turmeric

½–1 tsp chilli powder

1 tsp salt

1 green chilli, deseeded
and cut into strips

My Secrets

Before washing, spread the lentils out in a large tray to make it easier
to scan them for small stones and debris.

Check the lentils halfway through the final 12–15 minutes cooking
time. Pick up a few grains in a spoon and press them between your
forefinger and thumb. If they are tender at this stage, remove the lid
and increase the heat for quick evaporation of the excess water.

Bhuna Masaleki Machchi

Fish with stir-fried spices

Serves 4

8 large, fresh sardines, cleaned and gutted

salt and pepper

3 tbsp sunflower oil

½ tsp black mustard seeds

¼ tsp black onion seeds (ajowan)

1 medium onion, finely chopped

2.5 cm/1 in cube root ginger, finely grated

4 large cloves garlic, crushed

1 tsp fennel seeds

1 tsp ground coriander

½ tsp ground turmeric

½–1 tsp hot chilli powder

2 ripe tomatoes, skinned and chopped

½ fresh green chillies, deseeded and cut into julienne strips

2 tbsp coriander (cilantro) leaves, chopped

A quick and tasty dish for which you can use any firm-fleshed fish – River trout and small mackerel work well – as do shellfish such as large tiger prawns. For this recipe I have used fresh sardines with a delicious result. Allow at least 2 sardines per person.

In a smally heavy saucepan. heat the fennel seeds gently for 30 seconds and set aside to cool.

Wash the fish gently and pat dry. Season with salt and pepper and set aside.

In a non-stick frying pan, heat the oil over a medium heat, then add the fennel and onion seeds. Let them sizzle for a few seconds, then add the onion, ginger and garlic. Fry for 4–5 minutes then add 2 tablespoons of water.

Continue to cook until the onions are soft and light brown, then add the ground spices and cooked fennel seeds. Cook for 1 minute, then add 2 tablespoons of water. Cook until the water evaporates. Repeat this process with a further 2 tablespoons of water and allow to evaporate as before, then add the tomatoes and ¾ teaspoon salt, or to taste.

Cook until the tomatoes are pulpy and well incorporated into the spices. Add the fish, fresh chilli and coriander. Cover the pan and cook for 2–3 minutes. Carefully turn the fish over and cook for a further 2–3 minutes.

Remove from the heat and serve with plain boiled basmati rice and a lentil dish.

My Secrets

If you have some fresh dill, use this instead of coriander, as dill has a particular affinity with fish. However, if using dill, omit the ground fennel form the recipe.

Heating the whole spices until they pop and sizzle will bring out their full flavour and aroma. Heating the fennel seeds gently will activate the volatile oil which will add fabulous flavour to the dish.

Aam ka Gosht

Lamb with mango

Meat cooked with unripened or green mango, which has a sweet and sour taste, is a Mogul delicacy. As this type of mango is not yet easily available in the West, I created this new recipe using dried mango, which most supermarkets sell year round.

Remove and discard all visible fat from the meat, cut it into 5 cm/2 in cubes and set aside.

In a heavy saucepan, heat the oil over a medium-high heat and add the onion. Fry for 3–4 minutes, stirring constantly, then add the ginger and garlic and continue frying for another 3–4 minutes. Add the turmeric, cumin and chilli powder and stir-fry for 30 seconds. Then add 3 tablespoons of water and stir-fry until the water has evaporated. Repeat this process twice more.

Add the meat and reduce the heat to low. In a small bowl, whisk the yogurt and add it to the meat, mixing thoroughly. Cover the pan and cook for 40–45 minutes.

Add the tomatoes, mango and salt and simmer, uncovered, for 10–12 minutes. Increase the heat to medium-high and stir-fry for 2–3 minutes. Mix in the coriander (cilantro), lime juice and garam masala, remove from the heat and serve with any bread.

Instead of mango, you could use ready-to-eat dried apricots.

Serves 4

700 g/1½ lb boned shoulder of lamb

4 tbsp sunflower or soya oil

1 large onion, finely chopped

2.5 cm/1 in cube root ginger, peeled and grated

4–5 large cloves garlic, crushed

1 tsp ground turmeric

2 tsp ground cumin

½–1 tsp chilli powder

50 g/2 oz/¼ cup thick set plain yogurt

2 firm, ripe tomatoes, skinned and chopped

125 g/4 oz/½ cup dried mango

1 tsp salt, or to taste

2 tbsp coriander (cilantro) leaves, chopped

1½ tbsp lime juice

½ tsp garam masala

My Secret

The secret of successful Indian cooking lies in properly 'cooking out' the spices. They need to be fried to the stage where their raw taste is eliminated before meat, vegetables and so on are added.

Narangi Kheema

Minced meat with orange

Serves 4

3 tbsp sunflower or
vegetable oil

5 cm/2 in stick cinnamon

4 green cardamom pods

4 cloves

1 large onion, finely
chopped

2.5 cm/1 in cube root
ginger, finely grated

4–5 cloves garlic, crushed

1 tbsp ground coriander

½–1 tsp chilli powder

½ tsp ground turmeric

500 g/1 lb minced
(ground) lamb, beef or
pork

juice and finely grated zest
of 2 medium oranges

1 tsp salt, or to taste

½ tsp sugar

2 tbsp coriander (cilantro)
leaves, finely chopped

1–3 green chillies, sliced
lengthways

*For this refreshing dish, minced (ground) mutton is traditionally used
in India. I have tried it with lamb, beef and pork and each one has
produced its own distinctively delicious taste.*

In a heavy frying pan, heat the oil over a low-medium heat and add
the cinnamon, cardamom and cloves. Let them sizzle for 20–25
seconds. Add the onion, increase the heat slightly and fry, stirring
frequently, for 9–10 minutes or until the onion is light brown.

Stir in the ginger and garlic and continue frying for 1 minute, then
add the ground coriander, chilli powder and turmeric and fry for
1 minute. Mix in 2–3 tablespoons of water and fry for 1 minute.

Add the meat, increase the heat slightly and stir-fry for 6–7 minutes.
Sprinkle the mixture with 2–3 tablespoons of water and continue to
stir-fry for about 3–4 minutes until it is dry and the natural oil has
been released.

Add the orange juice and zest, salt and sugar. Reduce the heat to
low, cover the pan and cook for 10 minutes.

Add the fresh coriander (cilantro) and chillies and cook, uncovered,
for 3–4 minutes or until the mixture is dry, stirring frequently. Serve
with Palak Puri (Deep-fried bread with spinach), see page 130, or
Chukander ki Roti (Beetroot bread), see page 129.

My Secrets

The combination of meat and orange is very refreshing.

Using leftovers is an art which can be developed to create new
dishes. Indian housewives seem to excel in this area, perhaps
because of economic reasons and certain religious connotations.
Over the years, I have built on this practice and for this recipe I offer
you a delicious Kheema (minced meat) Pilau in case you have any
leftovers. Cook Mewa Pulao (Dry fruit pilau), see page 123, reheat
leftovers from this recipe and mix the two together. Serve with a
raita (salad).

Khargosh ka Kheema

Spicy minced hare

Here is a simple but superb recipe, born out of the passion for hunting among Mogul rulers. I have used rabbit in this recipe as it is more easily available. Buy boneless pieces of rabbit and mince (grind) it in the food processor. You could also use minced chicken.

In a bowl of cold water, soak the potatoes for 30 minutes, then drain and dry them thoroughly with a cloth.

Roughly chop the rabbit and place it in a food processor. Add the ginger, garlic, chilli, ground coriander, turmeric and yogurt. Blend until the mixture is fine, then set aside for 30 minutes.

In a large frying pan or skillet, heat 3 tablespoons of the oil over a low heat. Add the cardamom and cloves and fry them gently for 15–20 seconds. Add the marinated meat, stir well and let it cook, uncovered, for 18–20 minutes or until dry, stirring regularly.

Add the salt and chilli powder, increase the heat to medium and stir-fry for 2–3 minutes. Add 2–3 tablespoons of water and continue stir-frying until the mixture is dry. Repeat this once more. Add the tomato purée (paste), fresh coriander (cilantro) and mint. Remove the pan from the heat and keep it covered while you prepare the potatoes.

In a non-stick frying pan, heat the remaining oil over a medium heat. Add the potatoes and stir-fry them until beginning to brown. Reduce the heat slightly, cover the pan and cook for 3–4 minutes or until the potatoes are tender. Remove the lid and increase the heat again. Stir-fry until the potatoes are well browned, then sprinkle with the cumin and garam masala. Season to taste and remove from the heat.

Transfer the meat to a serving dish and top with the spiced potatoes. Garnish with the strips of fresh green chilli and serve with Palak Puri (Deep-fried bread with spinach), see page 130, or Chukander ki Roti (Beetroot bread), see page 129, and a raita.

My Secrets

The chefs at the Mogul palaces were as passionate about creating delectable game dishes as their masters were about hunting. With the help of a string of assistants, their job was easy!

We have to look for ways to save time and effort and in this instance, I start preparing and frying the potatoes while the mince is cooking.

Serves 4

1 large potato, about 225 g/8 oz, cut into bite-size pieces

500g/1 lb boneless rabbit portions

5 cm/2 in cube root ginger, roughly chopped

4–5 large cloves garlic, roughly chopped

1 green chilli, chopped

1 tbsp ground coriander

½ tsp ground turmeric

125 g/4 oz/½ cup whole milk plain yogurt

4 tbsp sunflower or soya oil

4 green cardamom pods, bruised

3 cloves

1 tsp salt, or to taste

½–1 tsp chilli powder

2 tsp tomato purée (paste)

2 tbsp coriander (cilantro) leaves, finely chopped

1 tbsp finely chopped mint leaves, or ½ tsp dried mint

½ tsp ground cumin

½ tsp garam masala

2 fresh green chillies, seeded and cut into strips

Kofta Bhuna

Stir-fried meatballs

Serves 4

1 large slice white bread, crusts removed

500 g/1 lb minced (ground) chicken or turkey

3 tbsp double (heavy) cream

1–2 green deseeded chillies

2 tbsp chopped mint leaves, or 1 tsp dried mint

6 large cloves garlic, roughly chopped

15 g/½ oz/¾ cup coriander (cilantro) leaves and stalks

5 cm/2 in cube root ginger, peeled and roughly chopped

1½ tsp garam masala

1½ tsp salt

1 large onion, roughly chopped

Meatballs made of minced (ground) chicken or turkey and whole new potatoes is a delicious dry but succulent dish. During the winter months, I like to serve this with Masala Puri (Deep-fried puffed bread), see page 126, for a warm and comforting feeling. A healthier alternative would be to serve it with boiled basmati rice and a lentil dish. Try and choose small new potatoes so that they are roughly the same size as the meatballs.

Cut the bread into pieces and place it in a food processor with the mince, cream, chillies and mint. Add 2 of the garlic cloves, half the coriander (cilantro) and half the ginger, ¾ teaspoon of the garam masala, ¾ teaspoon of salt. Blend the ingredients until smooth.

Divide the meatball mixture in half and use your hands to shape 8 equal-sized koftas out of each batch. Set aside.

Place the onion and the remaining garlic and ginger in a blender and process to a smooth purée, adding a little water if necessary.

Heat 1 tablespoon of the oil in a heavy non-stick frying pan or skillet over a medium-high heat. Working in batches, brown the meatballs, shaking the pan to turn the meatballs while cooking. Remove from the pan and set aside.

Reduce the heat to low and add the remaining 3 tablespoons of oil to the same pan. Fry the cinnamon and cardamom gently for 20–25 seconds, then add the puréed onion mixture, turmeric, chilli powder and ground coriander. Increase the heat to medium-high and stir-fry for 2–3 minutes. Add 3–4 tablespoons of water and continue to stir-fry for a further 2–3 minutes or until the water evaporates. Repeat this process once more.

My Secrets

When you are about to make the meatballs or koftas, have a bowl of water ready. Dip your palms into the bowl of water (this stops the mixture sticking to your hands) and rotate the koftas between the palms to make them smooth and round.

Watch the spices carefully so that you allow them to stick but not burn. Add the specified amount of water before they get a chance to burn. This is the secret that produces the unmistakably delicious toasted aroma in all bhuna dishes.

Add the tomatoes and the tomato purée (paste) and stir-fry for 4–5 minutes. Pour in 300 ml/½ pint/1¼ cups of warm water and the remaining ¾ teaspoon of salt. Add the meatballs and potatoes. Bring to the boil, then reduce the heat to low, cover the pan and simmer gently for 35–40 minutes or until the potatoes are tender.

Chop the remaining coriander (cilantro) leaves and stalks finely and add to the pan along with the remaining ¾ teaspoon of garam masala. Stir gently and cook, uncovered, for 1–2 minutes. Remove from the heat and serve.

4 tbsp sunflower or soya oil

5 cm/2 in stick cinnamon, halved

6 green cardamom pods, bruised

½ tsp ground turmeric

½–1 tsp chilli powder

1 tbsp ground coriander

175 g/6 oz/⅔ cup canned tomatoes, drained

1 tbsp tomato purée (paste)

500 g/1 lb small, even-sized new potatoes, scrubbed

Masaledar Kaleji

Spiced liver

Serves 4

1 large onion, roughly chopped

4 cloves garlic, roughly chopped

2.5 cm/1 in cube fresh ginger, roughly chopped

1 green chilli, chopped

4 tbsp sunflower or vegetable oil

500 g/1 lb lamb's liver, cut into 5 cm/2 in cubes

½–1 tsp chilli powder

1 tsp ground turmeric

2 tsp ground cumin

1 tsp ground coriander

125 g/4 oz/½ cup skinned and chopped fresh tomatoes or canned tomatoes in juice

1 tbsp tomato purée (paste)

2 tbsp coconut milk powder or creamed coconut, grated

1 tsp salt, or to taste

2 tbsp coriander (cilantro) leaves, chopped

½ tsp garam masala

Pieces of lamb's liver simmered in a rich tomato and onion sauce is rarely served in Indian restaurants in Britain. It is, however, a very popular dish in India, especially amongst the Muslims.

In a blender, purée the onion, garlic, ginger and chilli, adding a little water if necessary to make a paste. Set aside.

In a heavy non-stick frying pan, heat 1 tablespoon of the oil over a medium-high heat and add the liver and ½ teaspoon each of the chilli powder and turmeric. Fry for 5–6 minutes or until the juices run clear, stirring frequently. Remove the pan from the heat and transfer the liver to another dish.

Wipe the pan clean and heat the remaining oil over a medium heat. Add the puréed onion mixture and cook for 2–3 minutes. Add the remaining chilli powder and turmeric, cumin and ground coriander. Continue cooking for 4–5 minutes, stirring frequently.

Add the tomatoes and tomato purée (paste) and cook for 2–3 minutes. Mix in 4 tablespoons of water and continue to cook for a further 2–3 minutes. Meanwhile, blend the coconut milk powder or creamed coconut with 200 ml/7 fl oz/1 cup of hot water.

Add the fried liver, coconut milk and salt to the pan. Mix well and let it simmer gently until the liver is tender, about 20 minutes.

Stir in the coriander (cilantro) leaves and garam masala and remove from the heat. Serve with boiled basmati rice and a raita.

My Secrets

The precise moment at which the water is introduced to the barely sticking spices is crucial, but quite easy to identify. As soon as you can feel the spices just beginning to stick, add the water and continue stirring, scraping and mixing until you reach that stage again. I have seen my sister stirring and reaching for the water whilst reading a book!

For a really smooth sauce, use 175g/6 fl oz/¾ cup of passata (Italian sieved tomato) instead of fresh or canned tomatoes and reduce the quantity of tomato purée by half.

Bhuna Gosht
Meat with stir-fried spices

Although this dish originated in Northern India, Bhuna Gosht is popular all over the subcontinent. Lamb or mutton is used in the traditional recipe, but I have opted for beef for a change. Beef and mutton will need approximately the same cooking time but reduce the time by 10–15 minutes for lamb.

In a heavy-based saucepan, heat the oil over a medium heat and fry the onion, cinnamon, cloves and bay leaves for 7–8 minutes until the onion is soft.

Add the ginger, garlic, beef, spices and salt. Stir-fry over a medium heat for 10–12 minutes or until all the meat juices have evaporated. (Increase the heat to high if necessary.) Once the meat is dry, reduce the heat slightly and continue to fry for a further 6–8 minutes, adding 2–3 tablespoons of water whenever the spices start to stick to the bottom of the pan.

Add the whisked yogurt and cook for 1–2 minutes, then add the stock. Bring the mixture to the boil, reduce the heat to low, cover the pan and simmer for 45–50 minutes, or until the meat is tender.

Remove the lid and add the tomatoes. Stir-fry over a medium-high heat for 4–5 minutes until the tomatoes are well incorporated into the dish.

Sprinkle the garam masala over the dish and add the coriander (cilantro) leaves.

Stir-fry for 2–3 minutes, remove from the heat and serve with bread.

My Secret
To enhance the toasted aroma and taste of this dish, follow the guidelines given for temperature and timing in the initial frying process. Use a medium-sized saucepan so that the liquid does not evaporate too quickly during the simmering process.

Serves 4

4 tbsp sunflower oil

1 large onion, finely chopped

2.5 cm/1 in piece cinnamon stick

4 cloves

2 bay leaves

2.5 cm/1 in cube root ginger, finely grated

4–5 large cloves garlic, crushed

700 g/1½ lb/3¾ cups trimmed braising steaks, cut into 2.5 cm/1 in cubes

1 tsp ground turmeric

1 tsp chilli powder

2 tsp ground cumin

1 tsp salt, or to taste

125 g/4 oz/½ cup plain (whole milk) yogurt, whisked

175 ml/6 fl oz/¾ cup meat stock or warm water

200 g/7 oz/1 cup chopped canned tomatoes in juice

1 tsp garam masala

2–3 tbsp coriander (cilantro) leaves, chopped

Dum

Steaming

The delights of steam cooking

Dum is one of the easiest and most relaxed forms of cooking Indian food. Once the initial cooking process is over, the food is put into a heavy-based pan with a tight-fitting lid and the pan is sealed completely so that no steam can escape. Traditionally, a sticky dough made with flour and water is used to seal the pot which is then placed on hot charcoal. More burning charcoal is then put on top of the lid. It is necessary to be precise in judging the cooking time as the pot can be opened only when the food is fully cooked.

For Western kitchens, however, I have found a much easier and extremely effective way of preparing dum dishes and it is featured in the recipes in this chapter. I have worked out the precise timing for each recipe so all you have to do is follow them! Heavy saucepans with tight-fitting lids are absolutely necessary for dum cooking. You may need to buy a heat diffuser if your stove is not capable of giving a very low, steady heat. A bain marie is also useful for a gas or electric oven.

As I am not in favour of using excessive amounts of oil or butter in cooking, I have reduced the amount of fat to a much lower level than that traditionally used in dum dishes. This also necessitated adjusting the level of spicing and I am delighted with the lighter and fresher taste.

Dum Ki Subzi

Spiced steamed vegetables

Here is a wonderful combination of small new potatoes, green cabbage and shallots with simple flavouring and an easy cooking method. The natural flavours of all the vegetables can be enjoyed through the gentle but assertive taste of the spices.

In a heavy saucepan, heat the oil over a medium-low heat and add the shallots, ginger, garlic and chillies. Fry gently for 5–6 minutes.

Add the turmeric and chilli powder, if using, and cook for 30 seconds, then add all the remaining ingredients except the coriander (cilantro) leaves. Increase the heat to medium-high and stir-fry the vegetables for 2–3 minutes, then reduce the heat to very low and cover the pan with a piece of foil. Place the lid over the foil and seal the edges by folding the foil around the rim of the saucepan. Cook for 25–30 minutes or until the potatoes are tender. Remove the lid, add the coriander (cilantro) leaves and increase the heat slightly.

Cook for 1–2 minutes and remove from the heat. Serve with any bread accompanied by meat, fish or poultry dishes if desired.

Serves 4

2 tbsp sunflower or vegetable oil

225 g/8 oz/1 cup shallots, peeled and quartered

2.5 cm/1 in cube root ginger, finely grated

3 large cloves garlic, crushed

1–3 green chillies, finely chopped

½ tsp ground turmeric

½ tsp chilli powder (optional)

1 tsp salt

1 tsp sugar

300 g/10 oz small new potatoes, scrubbed

440 g/14 oz/1¾ cups green cabbage, finely shredded

2–3 tbsp coriander (cilantro) leaves, finely chopped

My Secrets

Boil the potatoes with their skins intact to retain the vitamins and flavour of the vegetable.

If there are no poppy seeds available, use ground sunflower seeds or pine nuts.

You can combine any vegetables of your choice in this dish. I remember my grandmother simply going out to the back garden to collect different types. She used to say that a combination of vegetables always produced better flavours than a single one.

Dum ke Aloo

Spiced baked potatoes

Serves 4

700 g/1½ lb small new potatoes, scrubbed

4 tbsp sunflower or vegetable oil

1 large onion, roughly chopped

2.5 cm/1 in cube root ginger, roughly chopped

2 tbsp white poppy seeds

75 g/3 oz/⅓ cup whole milk plain yogurt, whisked

1 tsp ground turmeric

1 tsp ground cumin

½–1 tsp chilli powder

½ tsp garam masala

1 tsp salt, or to taste

1–2 fresh green chillies, sliced

1–2 fresh red chillies, sliced

15 g/½ oz/¾ cup coriander (cilantro) leaves and stalks, finely chopped

2 tbsp fresh mint, finely chopped or 1 tsp dried mint

Potatoes have a marvellous affinity with spices. Boiled and pricked before cooking with spices, as in this recipe, enables the flavours to penetrate deeper inside the flesh. Indian housewives use this method regularly to transform the potatoes into a gourmet's delight.

Boil the potatoes until nearly tender, then drain and immerse in cold water. Prick the skin all over with a toothpick or fork and put them in a baking tray.

Preheat the oven to 190° C/375° F/Gas 5. Heat 1 tablespoon of the oil over a medium-high heat and stir-fry the onion and ginger for 3–4 minutes. Remove and let cool for a few minutes. Meanwhile, grind the poppy seeds until fine in a coffee or spice mill.

Put the yogurt in a blender and add the fried onion and ginger. Purée until smooth and transfer to a mixing bowl. Add the ground poppy seeds, turmeric, cumin, chilli powder, garam masala, salt and the remaining 3 tablespoons of oil. Mix thoroughly.

Pour the yogurt mixture over the potatoes in the baking tray and mix well. Cover with a piece of foil and bake on a high shelf for 10–12 minutes. Then reduce the temperature to 180° C/350° F/Gas 4 and bake for a further 7–8 minutes or until the potatoes are tender.

Remove the foil and add the chillies, coriander and mint. Mix well and return the potatoes, uncovered, to the oven. Bake for a further 3–4 minutes, sprinkling a little water over the potatoes if the spice mixture looks too dry – it should be clinging to the potatoes, which it will not do if too dry. Remove from the oven and serve with Roghani Roti (Creamy rich bread), see page 128, accompanied by Narangi Kheema (Minced meat with orange), see page 40, if liked.

Boiling the potatoes with the skin on retains vitamins and flavour.

My Secret

Although I like to use small new potatoes for this recipe, old potatoes produce a delicious result as well, even if one then has the extra chore of peeling them! Whatever potatoes you use, make sure they are all more or less uniform in size.

Badal Jaam

Spiced baked aubergine (eggplant)

This is a rather sophisticated style of cooking aubergines (eggplant) and the recipe originated in the royal kitchens of Northern India. Traditionally, the aubergine (eggplant) is sliced and deep-fried then topped with a delicious spicy tomato and onion mixture. This is my reduced fat version.

Preheat an overhead grill or broiler to high. Line a grill-pan with foil and brush it generously with oil. Slice the aubergines (eggplant) into 2.5 cm/ 1 in rounds (their diameter will vary). If you wish, soak them in salted water for 10–15 minutes to remove any bitterness, drain and rinse.

Pat the aubergines (eggplant) slices dry with a clean cloth. Place them on the prepared grill-pan, drizzle with 2 tablespoons of the oil and rub it in with your fingertips. Sprinkle with ½ teaspoon of salt and rub gently with your finger tips. Arrange the slices in a single layer and grill or broil them 15 cm/6 ins below the heat source for 4–5 minutes. Turn them over and grill for a further 4–5 minutes, then remove from the heat.

Preheat the oven to 190ºC/375ºF/Gas 5. Meanwhile, in a small saucepan, heat 2 tablespoons of oil over a medium heat and fry the onion for 5–6 minutes until softened. Add the ginger, garlic and chillies and fry for 1 minute. Add the cumin and tomato, cook for 1 minute and then stir in the mushrooms, tomato purée (paste), sugar and remaining salt. Reduce the heat to low and cook gently for 5 minutes.

Stir the coriander (cilantro) leaves into the tomato mixture, then remove it from the heat and divide it equally among the aubergine (eggplant) slices, spreading it over the surface. Cover with a piece of foil and bake in the centre of the oven for 15–20 minutes.

Using a flat spatula or fish slice, transfer the aubergine (eggplant) slices to a serving plate. Top with a heaped teaspoon of yogurt or crème fraîche and garnish with a little mint. Serve as an accompaniment to any meat, fish or poultry dishes with rice or bread.

Serves 4

2 aubergines (eggplant), about 250 g/9 oz each

4–5 tbsp sunflower or vegetable oil

1 tsp salt, or to taste

1 large onion, finely chopped

2.5 cm/1 in cube root ginger, finely grated

4–5 cloves garlic, crushed

1–2 green chillies, finely chopped

½ tsp ground cumin

1 medium tomato, skinned and chopped

90 g/3 oz/1 cup button mushrooms, sliced

1 tbsp tomato purée (paste)

¼ tsp sugar

2 tbsp coriander (cilantro) leaves and stalks, finely chopped

1 heaped tsp yogurt or crème fraîche

sprig of mint, to garnish

My Secrets

Choose aubergines (eggplant) that are lightweight and have a smooth, glossy, blemish-free skin. The lighter they are, the more they have of the wonderful velvety flesh and less of the seeds.

I normally omit the traditional soaking process for aubergines (eggplant) as modern varieties usually do not have any bitterness.

When grilling or broiling the aubergine (eggplant) slices, if they brown too much before they are cooked through, cover with a piece of foil for the last 1–2 minutes.

Sag Aloo
Spinach with potatoes

Serves 4

4 tbsp mustard or other cooking oil

½ tsp black mustard seeds

½ tsp cumin seeds

2 large garlic cloves, crushed

1 cm/½ in cube of root ginger, peeled and finely grated

1–2 fresh red chillies, cut at an angle, deseeded if liked

½ tsp ground turmeric

½ tsp chilli powder (optional)

700 g/1½ lb/4 cups potatoes, peeled and cut into 2/5 cm/1 in cubes

¾ tsp salt or to taste

225 g/8 oz/4 cups spinach leaves, chopped

This is my favourite spinach and potato recipe. My mother cooked it in pungent mustard oil, but you can use vegetable or corn oil. As for the dum (steaming), a piece of buttered greaseproof paper will work just as well in this recipe.

In a heavy pan, heat the oil over a medium heat. When hot but not smoking, add the mustard seeds. As soon as they pop, reduce the heat to low and add the cumin, then the garlic, ginger and chillies. Fry them gently until the garlic and ginger are slightly browned.

Stir in the turmeric and chilli powder (if using) then add the potatoes and salt. Sprinkle 3 tablespoons of water into the pan, stir then cover the potatoes with a piece of buttered greaseproof paper. Place the lid on the saucepan and reduce the heat to low. Cook for 7–8 minutes, stirring halfway through.

Add the spinach, stir and cover with the paper again and place the lid over the pan. Cook gently for 8–10 minutes until the vegetables are tender. Remove the lid and the buttered paper, stir and check that the spinach is clinging to the peices of potato. If there is much spinach juice left in the pan at this stage, reduce it gradually over a gentle heat with the lid off. Serve hot.

My secret
I like to garnish the dish with fried red onions. Because they are not cooked with the vegetables, the onions retain their fresh, vibrant colour. Fry them while the vegetables are cooking. Slice one large red onion finely and cook gently over a low-medium heat until softened, stirring regularly.

Tamatar ka Dulma
Stuffed tomatoes

Stuffed tomatoes, from the luxurious repertoire of the royal chefs of India, are delicious hot or cold and a reminder of bygone days of extravagance and indulgence. You can vary the stuffing by using small cauliflower florets, grated carrots, peas and so on. Here the mild, protein-rich Indian cheese paneer is used for the stuffing. You can use halloumi instead, a Greek cheese with a similar texture to Indian cheese, although if you do, remember to omit the salt from the recipe as this is very salty.

Preheat the oven to 190° C/375° F/Gas 5. Slice the tops off the tomatoes and reserve to use as lids. Scoop out the seeds and pulp and store for use in another recipe.

In a small saucepan, heat the oil over a medium-low heat and add the cumin seeds. Fry them gently for 15–20 seconds, then add the ginger and chillies and fry for 1 minute. Add the pistachios, raisins, turmeric and ground cumin. Cook for 1–2 minutes, then add all the remaining ingredients, mix well and remove from the heat.

Divide the mixture equally among the tomatoes and fill the cavities. Place the reserved lids on top and arrange the tomatoes in a greased roasting tin. Place a piece of foil over the top and seal the roasting tin completely by folding the edges of the foil all the way around the tin.

Bake in the centre of the oven for 15 minutes. Serve hot or cold as a vegetarian main meal with bread and lentils or vegetable curry. For meat eaters, team the stuffed tomatoes with kababs or tandoori food.

Serves 4

8 firm, medium tomatoes

1 tbsp sunflower or vegetable oil

½ tsp cumin seeds

1 cm/½in cube root ginger, finely grated

1–2 green chillies, finely chopped

1 tbsp raw pistachio nuts

1 tbsp seedless raisins

½ tsp ground turmeric

½ tsp ground cumin

125 g/4 oz/½ cup paneer or halloumi cheese, crumbled

½ tsp salt, or to taste

2 tbsp double (heavy) cream

2–3 tbsp coriander (cilantro) leaves, finely chopped

My Secrets

The jelly-like pulp which surrounds the seeds of the tomato is highly nutritious and flavoursome. Store the scooped-out tomato seeds and pulp in the fridge and use it in other dishes.

If you prefer, cashew nuts or blanched almonds are a great alternative to the pistachio nuts, although the colour they give to the dish is irreplaceable.

Lazeez Ghia Mussallam

Stuffed whole marrow

Serves 4–6

a large pinch of saffron strands, pounded

2 tbsp hot milk

1 medium marrow (squash)

1 tsp salt, or to taste

25 g/1 oz raw cashew pieces

25 g/1 oz sunflower seeds

4 tbsp sunflower or vegetable oil

1 large onion, roughly chopped

2.5 cm/1 in cube root ginger, finely grated

2-3 cloves garlic, crushed

125 g/4 oz/½ cup whole milk plain yogurt

125 g /4 oz/½ cup paneer or halloumi cheese, grated

2 green chillies, deseeded and finely chopped

This is an elegant vegetarian main meal that meat eaters can also enjoy in smaller quantities as a side dish. The marrow (squash) is hollowed out before stuffing. To make it easier, choose a marrow (squash) that is relatively straight.

Soak the pounded saffron in the hot milk and set aside.

Slice off both ends of the marrow (squash). Using an apple corer or medium-sized knife with a narrow blade, scoop out the seeds in a rotating movement, working from both ends of the vegetable to make it easier. Use a long handled spoon to scrape out any remaining seeds. Carefully peel the marrow (squash) and prick it all over with a fork. Rub in ½ teaspoon of the salt then leave to drain in a colander.

Preheat a small, heavy pan and dry-roast the cashews until brown spots begin to appear, stirring constantly. Add the sunflower seeds and roast for a further 1–2 minutes, stirring all the time. Remove them from the pan and spread on a plate to cool.

Preheat the oven to 190° C/375° F/Gas 5.

In a frying pan large enough to hold the marrow (squash), heat 2 tablespoons of the oil and fry the onion over a medium heat for 4–5 minutes. Add the ginger and garlic and continue frying for a further 2–3 minutes. Remove with a slotted spoon and transfer to a blender or food processor with the yogurt, saffron-infused milk, cashews and seeds. Blend to give a coarse mixture.

Transfer half the blended ingredients to a mixing bowl and add the cheese, ¼ teaspoon of salt (omit the salt if you are using halloumi), half the chillies, coriander (cilantro) and mint. Mix thoroughly and stuff the marrow (squash) with this mixture, leaving a 1 cm/½ in border at both ends so that the stuffing stays intact during cooking.

My Secrets

When buying marrow (squash), go for the ones with an even green coloured skin with no hint of brown or yellow. To serve the stuffed marrow (squash), use a carving knife and fork to cut it into thick slices. Lift the slices gently and carefully.

Once the marrow (squash) was peeled, my mother would deftly create wonderful recipes with the skin cut into neat pieces. As the skin is full of vitamins and other nutrients, I often follow her example and cook it simply in olive oil, garlic, chillies and a touch of turmeric. Add salt to taste and sweat the marrow (squash) skin until tender.

Add another 2 tablespoons of oil to the pan and heat over a high heat. Brown the stuffed marrow, carefully turning it around and over in the pan, then switch off the heat and transfer the marrow to a deep roasting tin.

Place the pan in which the marrow was browned over a low heat and add the chilli powder, ground coriander and garam masala. Cook for 30 seconds, then add the tomato purée (paste) and cook for 1–2 minutes. Add the remaining yogurt paste, chillies, coriander, mint and 125 ml/4 fl oz/½ cup of lukewarm water. Add the last ¼ teaspoon of salt (or adjust the salt to taste if you are using halloumi). Mix well and remove from the heat.

Pour the curried mixture over the prepared marrow and spread it round the sides. Cover the roasting tin with a piece of foil and bake in the centre of the oven for 20–25 minutes. Remove and carefully transfer the marrow to a serving dish. If a little of the stuffing spills out, simply push it back in with a spoon. Mix the thickened spice paste with the cooking juices, spread it all over the marrow and serve with any bread.

15 g/½ oz/¾ cup coriander (cilantro) leaves and stalks, finely chopped

2 tbsp finely chopped fresh mint, or 1 tsp dried mint

½–1 tsp chilli powder

1 tsp ground coriander

½ tsp garam masala

2 tbsp tomato purée (paste)

Batair Mussallam

Stuffed quails

Serves 4

For the stuffed quails:

4 quails

50 g/2 oz/¼ cup paneer or halloumi cheese, grated

15 g/½ oz seedless raisins

2 ready-to-eat dried apricots, finely chopped

1 tsp fresh ginger, finely grated

1–2 green chillies, deseeded and finely chopped

1 tbsp coriander (cilantro) leaves, finely chopped

½ tsp salt

1 tbsp single (light) cream

For the sauce:

2 tbsp white poppy seeds

1 tbsp coriander seeds

The Mogul emperors and princes were passionate about hunting, so the palace chefs created a delectable range of game recipes for the Mogul tables. This is my creation, but using the guidelines set out in the traditional Mogul cooking. Traditionally, the skin is removed, but, as these are such tiny birds, I feel it's not worth the effort. It is a little time-consuming to prepare but don't be put off as it is worth all the effort you put into it.

Clean the quails and wipe them inside and out. Score the skin, making a few incisions in the flesh at the same time.

In a bowl, mix all the stuffing ingredients well and divide them into 4 equal portions. Stuff the cavities of the quails with this mixture, pushing it up as far as possible. Truss the birds with tooth picks or trussing needles.

To begin the sauce, grind the white poppy seeds, coriander and sesame seeds, dried red chillies and mace in a coffee grinder or spice mill until fine. Transfer the spice mixture to a bowl and stir in the turmeric. Set aside.

In a large heavy saucepan, heat the oil over a low heat and add the cardamom and cinnamon. Sizzle for 35–40 seconds, then add the onion, ginger and garlic and fry for 7–8 minutes or until the onion is soft, stirring frequently.

Add the ground spice mixture and continue cooking for 1 minute. Stir in the yogurt and salt and cook for 2–3 minutes. Pour in 125 ml/4 fl oz/½ cup of lukewarm water and stir well.

My Secret

To make a smooth garlic pulp quickly, place the chopped garlic on a flat surface and add the salt intended for the recipe. Crush with a wooden pestle or the back of a wooden spoon – the blade of a large knife works very well too. You can crush the garlic and ginger together if you chop the ginger into small pieces first.

Add the stuffed quails and turn them around in the pan until they are coated with the spices, then sit the birds close together in the pan, breast side down. Turn the heat to very low.

Soak a piece of greaseproof paper in some water and then squeeze it out. Place it on top of the saucepan, making sure it is not touching the birds. Cover with the lid and cook for 20 minutes.

Remove the lid, turn the birds on their backs and re-cover as before with the greaseproof paper and the lid. Cook for a further 20 minutes. To test if the birds are done, prick the thighs with a fork to see if the juices are running clear and, if not, cook for a few minutes longer. Serve with naan.

1 tbsp sesame seeds

2–3 dried red chillies, chopped

½ blade mace

½ tsp ground turmeric

3 tbsp sunflower or soya oil

4 green cardamom pods, bruised

5 cm/2 in stick cinnamon, halved

1 medium onion, finely chopped

2.5 cm/1 in cube root ginger, finely grated

4 large cloves garlic, crushed

125 g/4 oz/½ cup whole milk yogurt

Dum Machchi

Fish baked in an aromatic sauce

Serves 4

700 g/½lb firm, chunky white fish fillets or steaks

1½ tbsp lime juice

1 tsp salt

2.5 cm/1 in stick cinnamon, broken

seeds of 6 green cardamom pods

1 tsp cumin seeds

2 tsp coriander seeds

1 tbsp white poppy seeds

1 tbsp sunflower seeds

4 tbsp sunflower or vegetable oil

1 large onion, very finely chopped

4 large cloves garlic, crushed

2.5 cm/1 in cube root ginger, finely grated

½–1 tsp chilli powder

½ tsp ground turmeric

125 g/4 oz/½ cup whole milk plain yogurt, whisked

2 medium tomatoes, sliced

2–3 tbsp coriander (cilantro) leaves, finely chopped

I have vivid memories of visiting fish markets with my mother where the fishmongers would have the daily catch, some of which would still be alive and jumping! My mother would promptly buy these and then go about choosing the freshest ones possible from the rest. She would ask me to gently press the fish to see if it would spring back, which is a sign of absolute freshness.

Cut the fish fillets or steaks into 2–3 pieces. Sprinkle the lime juice and half the salt, rub in gently and set aside for 20 minutes.

Preheat the oven to 150°C/300°F/Gas 2. Meanwhile, grind the cinnamon, cardamom seeds, cumin, coriander, poppy and sunflower seeds in a coffee or spice mill until fine. Set aside.

In a small saucepan, heat the oil over a medium heat and add the onion. Fry until soft and translucent but not brown. Add the garlic and ginger and continue frying for 2 minutes, then add the ground ingredients, plus the chilli powder and turmeric. Cook, stirring constantly, for 1 minute. Add the remaining ½ teaspoon of salt and the yogurt. Mix thoroughly and remove from the heat.

In a roasting tin measuring about 37.5 cm/15 in x 30 cm/12 in, spread half the cooked spice mixture, half the sliced tomatoes and half the coriander (cilantro) leaves. Arrange the fish on top in a single layer. Carefully spread the remaining spice mix, coriander leaves and tomatoes on top. Cover the tin with a piece of foil and seal the edges completely by pressing the foil all the way around the rim of the tin. Bake in the centre of the oven for 35–40 minutes.

Carefully transfer the fish to a serving dish and pour any remaining cooking juices over the fish. Serve with Kesar Pulao (Saffron pilau), see page 121, and a vegetable dish.

My Secrets

Choose firm fish such as monk, shark or red mullet for this superbly flavoured dish. Chunky cod, haddock or halibut can also be used if you handle them carefully – they tend to flake easily.

An easy way to enhance the flavour of this is to let the spice layered fish stand for at least an hour before placing it in the oven.

Dum ki Nalli

Slow-cooked lamb shanks

Tender, delicious and opulent is the only way to describe these lamb shanks. The dish is easy to cook and makes a luxurious special occasion dinner with Sheermal (Milk bread), see page 127, and Mewa ka Raita (Dry fruit and nuts in yogurt), see page 144.

Remove any excess fat and membrane from the lamb shanks and wipe them with a clean cloth. Preheat a small, heavy pan, griddle or skillet over a medium heat. When hot, reduce the heat to low, add the sunflower seeds and roast them gently until they begin to brown. Add the poppy seeds and continue to roast, stirring constantly, for 30–40 seconds. Transfer the seeds to a plate to cool. Whisk the yogurt until smooth and set aside.

Heat the oil in a heavy saucepan over a medium heat and fry the onion, stirring frequently, for 10–12 minutes or until soft and light golden in colour. Add the ginger and garlic and continue frying for 1–2 minutes.

Add the chilli powder, turmeric, coriander and half the garam masala and fry for 1 minute. Add 2 tablespoons of the whisked yogurt and cook for 2 minutes. Then add the lamb shanks, the remaining yogurt, salt and 300 ml/½ pint/1¼ cups of lukewarm water. Mix well and bring the mixture to a slow simmer. Cover the pan with double thickness of foil, making sure it does not touch the food, then cover with the lid. Seal the edges by pressing the foil into the saucepan rim. Reduce the heat to low and simmer gently for 30 minutes.

Meanwhile, grind the roasted seeds in a coffee grinder or spice mill until smooth. When the shanks have been cooking for 30 minutes, add the ground seeds to the saucepan and mix well. Cover as before with the foil and lid and continue to cook gently for a further 25–30 minutes.

Whent the meat is tender it is cooked. Stir in the remaining garam masala and lemon juice and remove from the heat.

Serves 4

4 lamb shanks

3 tbsp sunflower seeds

2 tbsp white poppy seeds

175 g/6 oz/¾ cup whole milk plain yogurt

4–5 tbsp sunflower or soya oil

1 large onion, finely chopped

5 cm/2 in cube root ginger, finely grated

4–5 large cloves garlic, crushed

½–1 tsp chilli powder

½ tsp ground turmeric

1 tbsp ground coriander

1½ tsp garam masala

1 tsp salt, or to taste

1 tbsp lemon juice

My Secret
Be sure to keep the heat at a steady low level while adding the yogurt, or it may separate or curdle.

Shabdegh

Slow-cooked lamb with turnips

Serves 4

500 g/1 lb small turnips

1 large onion

50 g/2 oz/¼ cup blanched almonds

1 slice large white bread, crusts removed

500 g/1 lb lean minced (ground) lamb or beef

2 tbsp double (heavy) cream

1 tsp garam masala

2 tbsp mint leaves, finely chopped

3 tbsp coriander (cilantro) leaves, finely chopped

1–2 green chillies, deseeded and finely chopped

7.5 cm/3 in cube root ginger, finely grated

8 large cloves garlic, crushed

4 tbsp sunflower or soya oil

This delectable dish consists of turnips with both cubed lamb and lamb meatballs. Traditionally the three ingredients, with herbs, spices and a large amount of ghee, were left to cook together through the night (shab) in a sealed pan known as 'degh', hence the Indian name. This is my adaptation with a shortened cooking time and no ghee, but the result is quite splendid.

Preheat the oven to 220°C/425°F/Gas 7. Peel the turnips and put them in a roasting tin. Peel and cut the onion into large chunks and place them alongside the turnips. Place the almonds on one side of the roasting tin. With your fingertips, rub a little oil into these ingredients, but keep them apart from each other. Place the roasting tin on a high shelf in the oven and set the timer for 7 minutes. Remove the almonds and continue to roast the onion and turnips for a further 7–8 minutes until they are golden brown. Remove and set aside to cool.

Cut the bread into cubes and place it in a food processor with the minced (ground) meat, cream, garam masala, mint, coriander leaves (cilantro) and green chillies. Add 1 teaspoon each of the grated ginger and crushed garlic and process until the mixture is smooth. Have a bowl of water ready to moisten your palms, then shape the meat mixture into 14 equal-sized meatballs, rotating them between your palms until smooth and round.

In a non-stick frying pan, heat 1 tablespoon of the oil over a medium heat and fry the meatballs until they are browned, occasionally shaking the pan from side to side so that they can brown evenly. Remove them with a slotted spoon and set aside.

My Secret

This is a wonderful dinner party or special occasion recipe. To prepare it ahead, the three main steps can be completed a day or two earlier. I prepare the roasted ingredients, fry the meatballs and make the almond purée and store them in the fridge. This way, all I have to do on the day of the event is prepare the cubed meat and then leave everything to take care of itself for 1½ hours.

Place the roasted onion and almonds in a blender. Add 225 ml/
8 fl oz/1 cup of water and blend to a smooth purée. Set aside.

In a heavy saucepan, heat the remaining oil over a low heat and add
the royal cumin seeds and cardamom pods. Let them sizzle gently
for 20–25 seconds, then add the remaining ginger and garlic and fry
for 30 seconds. Add the cubed meat, chopped onion, chilli powder,
nd turmeric. Increase the heat to medium-high and fry the meat for
6–7 minutes or until browned, stirring frequently.

Reduce the heat to low and add the whisked yogurt, salt, roasted
turnips, fried meatballs and the almond purée. Mix gently but
thoroughly and cover the pan with a piece of foil. Press the foil all
around the edges of the saucepan to seal it completely and cover
with the lid. After 4–5 minutes, check the saucepan lid to see if it is
really hot, then reduce the heat to the lowest possible setting. Cook
for 1½ hours, shaking the pan from side to side at least 3–4 times
during cooking. Remove from the heat and serve with Jeera Chawal
(Cumin Flavoured Rice), see page 120, or boiled basmati rice.

1 tsp royal cumin seeds
(shahi jeera)

6 green cardamom pods,
bruised

500 g/1 lb lamb leg meat
or braising steak, cut into
2.5cm/1 in cubes

1 small onion, finely
chopped

½–1 tsp chilli powder

½ tsp ground turmeric

150 g/5 oz/⅔ cup whole
milk plain yogurt, whisked

1–1½ tsp salt

Noor Mahal Biryani

Rice steamed with aromatic lamb

Serves 6

A large pinch of saffron strands, pounded

2 tbsp hot milk

250 g/9 oz lean minced (ground) lamb or beef

7.5 cm/3 in cube root ginger, finely grated

8 large cloves garlic, crushed

125 g/4 oz/½ cup whole milk plain yogurt, whisked

2½ tsp salt

1 green chilli, deseeded and finely chopped

2 tbsp coriander (cilantro) leaves, finely chopped

1 tbsp fresh mint, finely chopped or ½ teaspoon dried mint

½ tsp garam masala

4 tbsp ghee or unsalted butter

1 large onion, finely sliced

Developed during the Mogul reign in Agra, where the exquisite Taj Mahal is the centre (noor) of attention, this biryani is one of the most popular among the exotic range created in the royal kitchens. In India, such exotic biryanis are the central attraction at dinner parties. The word biryani means a layered rice dish cooked by steaming.

In a small bowl, soak the pounded saffron in the hot milk and set aside.

Put the minced (ground) meat into a mixing bowl and 1 teaspoon each of the grated ginger and crushed garlic. Mix well, then add 2 tablespoons of the yogurt, ½ teaspoon of the salt, the chilli, fresh coriander (cilantro), mint and garam masala. Knead the mixture until smooth and shape into 12 equal-sized koftas or meatballs. Set aside.

In a heavy saucepan, melt the ghee or butter over a medium heat and fry the onion for 10–12 minutes or until it is a light golden colour, reducing the heat slightly if necessary. Switch off the heat source and lift the onions with a slotted spoon, pressing down with another spoon to squeeze the excess fat back into the pan. Drain the onions on absorbent paper.

Turn the heat source on to medium and in the same pan brown the meatballs, turning them gently to encourage even browning. Drain on absorbent paper.

Reduce the heat to low and add half the quantities of cinnamon, cardamom, cloves and bay leaves to the remaining fat. Allow them to sizzle gently for 20–25 seconds, then add the remaining ginger and garlic and fry gently for 1 minute. Add the coriander and cumin and continue to cook gently for about 1 minute.

My Secret
Sealing the pot completely produces plenty of vapour or steam inside. The food is cooked gently and slowly in the vapour. This method enhances the development and blending of the individual flavours of the spices.

Add the meat, increase the heat to medium and fry for 2–3 minutes. Add the remaining yogurt and ½ teaspoon of the salt and mix thoroughly. Sprinkle half the rose water and half the fried onion over the meat. Switch off the heat source and keep the pan covered while you prepare the rice.

In another large saucepan or flameproof casserole, bring plenty of water to the boil and add the remaining salt, cinnamon, cardamom, cloves and bay leaves. Add the rice and bring back to the boil. Let it boil steadily for 2–3 minutes, then drain the rice, making sure that you do not discard the whole spices.

Pile the rice on top of the meat and level the surface with a spoon. Sprinkle the remaining rose water and fried onion over the rice and arrange the fried meatballs on top.

Soak a clean tea towel in hand-hot water and wring out. Place it on top of the biriyani, then cover the saucepan with a double thickness of foil. Press the foil all the way around the edges of the saucepan to seal it completely, then put the lid on. Place the pan over a very low heat (using a heat diffuser if necessary) and cook for 1 hour. Alternatively, if using an ovenproof saucepan or casserole, place in the centre of a preheated oven (170°C/325°F/Gas 3) for 1 hour.

Switch off the heat source and let the cooked biriyani stand undisturbed for 10–12 minutes. Serve with a raita and grilled or fried pappodums.

4 x 2.5 cm/1 in sticks cinnamon

8 green cardamom pods, bruised

8 cloves

4 bay leaves

1½ tbsp ground coriander

1 tbsp ground cumin

500 g/1 lb boned leg of lamb or braising steak, trimmed of fat and cut into 5 cm/2 in cubes

2 tbsp rose water

500 g/1 lb basmati rice, washed and drained

Korma

Braising

The captivating korma

Korma, which means braising, is one of the most important techniques in Indian cooking and produces alluring flavours. It is a total misconception that kormas are always rich and creamy. There are different types of kormas, some quite rich and luxurious, others that are light and aromatic. Some are pale, creamy and mild but those with a fiery looking appearance have a taste to match. The difference lies in the regional practice of combining and blending the spices. Kormas are traditionally meat-based dishes, but vegetarian versions are now more common.

Richer kormas are normally marinated in a spice-laced creamy yogurt mixture and braised very slowly in ghee. Shahi korma is a classic example of this category. The word shahi means 'royal' and its origin lies in the royal kitchens of India. No Mogul emperor's dinner table was complete without a shahi korma.

The popular do-piaza is a form of korma but has a lighter taste as it does not contain any cream or nut paste. My mother knew how to cook a do-piaza to perfection. I remember drooling over her strikingly beautiful, vibrantly red sauce that coated succulent pieces of firm river fish, freshly caught large prawns or tender pieces of young chicken. She always used two types of onions in her coarse paste-like do-piaza mixture, making it visually appealing as well as giving a delightful taste.

No matter which type of korma you want to make, always use prime quality meat. Braising meat is ideal for the slow cooking method, but you should avoid the stewing cuts. To get the best results, your pots and pans should be as heavy as possible and always have tight-fitting lids. The size of the saucepan is also very important in cooking a successful korma: it should not be too big or too small, but just large enough to hold the meat comfortably.

Subzion ka Korma
Vegetable korma

The korma style of cooking was originally used only for meat and poultry but its popularity is so overwhelming that various vegetarian recipes have been created in recent years. My creation is a subtle sensation of flavours and a visual delight.

Soak the almonds in 150 ml/5 fl oz/⅔ cup of boiling water for 20 minutes.

In a heavy saucepan, heat the oil over a medium heat and add the onions. Fry them for about 10–12 minutes until light brown, stirring frequently.

Add the chillies and ginger and fry for 1 minute, then add the coriander, turmeric and chilli powder. Reduce the heat to low and fry for 2 minutes. Add the tomato purée (paste) and 2 tablespoons of water and continue cooking for 2–3 minutes.

Add the potatoes, carrots, green beans, salt and sugar. Pour in 450 ml/16 fl oz/2 cups of lukewarm water, stir once and bring to the boil. Cover the pan and simmer for 10 minutes.

Meanwhile, in a blender, purée the almonds with the water in which they were soaked. Add this mixture to the vegetables along with the cream, then cover and simmer for 5 minutes.

Add the cauliflower, cover and simmer for a further 5–6 minutes or until all the vegetables are tender but still firm. Serve with Lasoon ki Roti (Garlic bread), see page 131, or Roghani Roti (Creamy rich bread), see page 128.

My Secrets
Like choosing the choice cuts of meat, a vegetable korma too deserves the finest and freshest produce.

Always use a combination of 3 vegetables. Choose them carefully so that the colours, textures and tastes compliment each other.

Serves 4

50 g/2 oz/¼ cup blanched almonds

4 tbsp sunflower or soya oil

2 medium onions, finely sliced

2 green chillies, deseeded and sliced

2.5 cm/1 in cube root ginger, finely grated

1 tbsp ground coriander

½ tsp ground turmeric

½ tsp chilli powder

1 tbsp tomato purée (paste)

375 g/12 oz/1½ cups potatoes, peeled and cut into 2.5 cm/1 in cubes

125 g/4 oz/½ cup carrots, cut into batons

125 g/4 oz/½ cup fine green beans (haricots verts), cut into 5 cm/2 in pieces

1½ tsp salt, or to taste

½ tsp sugar

125 ml/4 fl oz/½ cup single (light) cream

375 g/12 oz/1½ cups cauliflower florets, about 1 cm/1½ in in diameter

Machchi Korma
Fish korma

Serves 4

4 large salmon steaks,
700 g/1½ lb in total

1 tbsp lemon juice

1 tsp salt

50 g/2 oz/¼ cup raw
cashew nuts

3 tbsp sunflower or soya
oil

5 cm/2 in stick cinnamon,
halved

4 green cardamom pods,
bruised

2 cloves

1 large onion, finely
chopped

1–2 green chillies,
deseeded and finely
chopped

2.5 cm/1 in cube root
ginger, finely grated

2–3 large cloves garlic,
crushed

150 ml/5 fl oz/⅔ cup single
(light) cream

50 g/2 oz/¼ cup whole milk
plain yogurt

½ tsp ground turmeric

1 tsp sugar

Generally, Indian fish have quite a firm texture and can easily be simmered in sauces without disintegrating. I like to use salmon steaks for this recipe. The pink flesh of the salmon looks quite spectacular in the pale background of the sauce, while the subtle flavour of the sauce complements the delicate flavour of the fish perfectly. The importance of fish cooked and eaten in peak condition could not have been more evident than in the royal kitchens of India. The chefs had the fish, caught in the morning, delivered straight to the royal kitchen door. It would come covered in a tray with the edges completely sealed with a dough!

Cut each salmon steak in half lengthways. Put them on a large plate and gently rub in the lemon juice and ½ teaspoon of salt. Set aside for 20 minutes.

Soak the cashews in boiling water for 15 minutes.

Heat the oil in a wide shallow pan over a low heat and add the cinnamon, cardamom and cloves. Sizzle for 30–40 seconds. Add the onion, chillies, ginger and garlic. Increase the heat slightly and fry, stirring frequently, for 9–10 minutes or until the onions are very soft.

Meanwhile, drain the cashews and purée them with the cream and the yogurt.

Stir the turmeric into the onion mixture and add the cashew cream, ½ teaspoon of salt and the sugar. Mix thoroughly, then arrange the fish in the sauce in a single layer. Bring to a simmer, cover the pan and cook for 5 minutes.

Remove the lid and shake the pan gently from side to side. Spoon some of the sauce over the fish pieces. Cover again and continue cooking for a further 3–4 minutes. Remove and serve with Kesar Pulao (Saffron pilau), see page 121, if liked.

My Secret
Most fish found in Britain is quite flaky and, therefore, you need to be very careful when choosing one for an Indian dish that involves simmering in sauce.

Besides salmon, you could also use rainbow trout, but shoose small, whole fish rather than fillets. Lightly score each fish to allow the flavours to penetrate.

Jhinge ka Korma

Prawn (shrimp) korma

This is a real feast for prawn lovers, and they include me! The peeled and cooked prawns(shrimp) are simply heated through in a small quantity of superbly flavoured sauce. Eat to your heart's content with Sheermal (Milk bread), see page 127, or Roghani Roti (Creamy rich bread), see page 128, or boiled basmati rice.

In a large mixing bowl, combine the prawns (shrimp), lemon juice and turmeric, mix and set aside. Whisk the yogurt and besan together and set aside.

Grind the sunflower and poppy seeds in a coffee or spice mill until fine. Empty into a bowl, mix with the ground almonds and set aside.

In a heavy saucepan, heat the oil over a medium heat and add the onion. Fry for 6–7 minutes or until the onion is soft and translucent. Add the ginger, garlic and green chillies and continue frying for 2–3 minutes. Mix in the ground seed mixture and chilli powder and cook for 2–3 minutes, stirring constantly.

Add the prawns (shrimp), whisked yogurt and salt, reduce the heat to low, cover the pan and cook for 3–4 minutes until the prawns are heated through. Stir in the coriander (cilantro) leaves and remove from the heat.

Serves 4–5

800 g/1¾ lb prawns (shrimp), thawed and drained if frozen

3 tbsp lemon juice

½ tsp ground turmeric

150 g/5 oz/⅔ cup whole milk plain yogurt

1½ tsp besan (gram flour)

2 tbsp sunflower seeds

2 tbsp white poppy seeds

2 tbsp ground almonds

4 tbsp sunflower or vegetable oil

1 large onion, finely chopped

2.5 cm/1 in cube root ginger, finely grated

4–5 large cloves garlic, crushed

1–3 green chillies, deseeded and finely chopped

½–1 tsp chilli powder

1½ tsp salt, or to taste

3 tbsp coriander (cilantro) leaves and stalks, finely chopped

My Secret
Frozen prawns (shrimp) will retain maximum flavour if they are thawed slowly, preferably in the fridge for 24 hours. Drain off all the liquid before using.

Murgh Korma Mussallam

Korma of stuffed whole chicken

Serves 4

For the birds:

2 poussins, about 400 g/ 14 oz each

50g/2oz/¼ cup plain Greek yogurt

1 tbsp lemon juice

5 cm/2 in cube root ginger, finely grated

4–5 large cloves garlic, crushed

½–1 tsp chilli powder

½ tsp ground turmeric

salt

For the stuffing:

1 tbsp sunflower or soya oil

1 small onion, finely chopped

2.5 cm/1 in cube root ginger, finely grated

1–3 green chillies, deseeded and finely chopped

125 g/4 oz/½ cup paneer or halloumi cheese, grated

Kormas are generally served on special occasions because they tend to be quite rich. The other reason is that only young, quality meat is used to cook them and this comes with a much higher price tag. For this recipe, you need prime young chicken to match the delightful taste and flavour of the sauce and the fruit and nut stuffing. I have chosen poussins, but you could use a small free range chicken. Two poussins are more than sufficient for four people; serve with Sada Pulao (Plain pilau rice), see page 119, or Kesar Pulao (Saffron pilau), see page 121, for a sumptuous meal.

Skin the poussins. Wipe them with a damp cloth inside and out, then prick all over with a fork. Mix the yogurt with 1 teaspoon of salt, plus the lemon juice, ginger, garlic, chilli powder and turmeric. Rub the mixture well into the birds and refrigerate in a covered container for 4–6 hours or overnight. Bring to room temperature before stuffing the birds.

To prepare the stuffing, heat the oil over a low heat and fry the onion, ginger and chillies for 4–5 minutes or until the onion is soft. Remove from the heat and add all the remaining ingredients. Stuff the stomach cavity of the birds generously with this mixture, reserving a little of the stuffing to add to the sauce later. Tie up the birds with string in a criss cross fashion.

To make the sauce, in a heavy saucepan, heat the ghee or butter over a low heat and add the cardamom, cinnamon and dried red chillies. Fry them gently for 15–20 seconds, then add the onion and fry for 4–5 minutes until the onion is soft. Place the birds side by side on their backs in the pan and spread any remaining marinade over them.

My Secrets

If you don't have Greek yogurt, which is ideal because of its creaminess, then you can use natural yogurt if the water content is removed first. Do this by pouring the yogurt into muslin, tie it with a piece of string and leave to hang for an hour per 225 g/8 oz.

When covering the pan with foil, leave enough of a gap between the birds and the foil. The moisture collected on the inner roof of the foil will trickle down onto the birds, keeping them moist and succulent.

Cover the pan with a double thickness of foil and place the lid on top. Seal the rim of the saucepan by pressing the foil into it. Reduce the heat to very low and cook for 25–30 minutes. Turn the birds over, cover again with the foil and lid, and continue cooking for a further 25–30 minutes.

Remove the lid and foil and turn the birds over again on their backs. Spoon some of the sauce over them and add any leftover stuffing to the sauce. Cook for 3–4 minutes, increasing the heat slightly, if necessary, to thicken the sauce. Remove and serve.

2 tbsp double (heavy) cream

2–3 ready-to-eat dried apricots, finely chopped

25 g/1 oz/2 tbsp pine nuts

1½ tsp white poppy seeds, crushed

2–3 tbsp coriander (cilantro) leaves, finely chopped

For the sauce:

2 tbsp ghee or unsalted butter

4 green cardamom pods, bruised

5 cm/2 in stick cinnamon, halved

1–2 dried red chillies, chopped

1 small red onion, finely chopped

Saphed Korma Murgh
White chicken korma

Serves 4

50 g/2 oz/¼ cup blanched almonds

2.5 cm/1 in stick cinnamon, broken

seeds of 6 green cardamom pods

2 tsp coriander seeds

1½ tbsp white poppy seeds

250 g/9 oz/1 cup whole milk plain yogurt

2.5 cm/1 in cube root ginger, finely grated

4–5 large cloves garlic, crushed

1 tsp salt, or to taste

½ tsp freshly ground white pepper

700 g/1½ lb/3 cups skinless chicken breast fillets, cut into 5 cm/2 in cubes

4 tbsp ghee or unsalted butter

2–3 green chillies, halved lengthways, deseeded if wished

2 tbsp rose water

a few soft pink unsprayed rose petals, to garnish (optional)

This recipe is from the colourful princely state of Rajasthan (abode of the Kings) in North Western India. Nothing that may add even a hint of colour is used in this dish.

Place the almonds in a bowl, cover with 125 ml/4 fl oz/½ cup of boiling water and soak for 15 minutes.

Preheat a small heavy pan over a low heat for about 1 minute, then add the cinnamon, cardamom and coriander seeds. Stir until they begin to release their aroma, about 30 seconds, then add the poppy seeds and switch off the heat. Keep stirring for a further 30 seconds, then let the ingredients cool. Grind them finely in a coffee grinder or spice mill and set aside.

In a small bowl, whisk the yogurt until smooth. Mix in the ginger, garlic, salt and white pepper and set aside.

Put the chicken in a heavy saucepan and add the roasted ground spices, yogurt mixture and the ghee or butter. Mix thoroughly and place the pan over low heat to warm through for a few minutes.

Meanwhile, purée the almonds with the water in which they were soaked and add to the chicken. Cover the pan with double thickness of foil, then cover with the lid. Seal the pan by crumpling the edges of the foil all around the saucepan rim. Wait for 5 minutes and check that the saucepan lid is hot, then turn the heat to the lowest setting and cook for 25–30 minutes.

Add the chillies and stir in the rose water. Recover the pan with foil, put on the lid and switch off the heat. Let the korma stand for 10–15 minutes to allow the chillies' flavour to infuse the sauce. Remove the chillies before serving, garnished with rose petals if using and accompanied by Sada Pulao (Plain pilau rice), see page 119.

My Secret
For an exotic look, I like to sprinkle the pieces of chicken with silver dust to mimic the edible silver leaves that adorned the chicken during the Mogul era. You can buy silver dust from specialist shops which sell ingredients for cake decorating.

Firdausi Qorma

Heavenly korma

When I visited my family in New Delhi recently, I took my usual trip to Karim's, one of my favourite restaurants and one of the oldest in town. Situated in Old Delhi, it was founded by an extraordinary chef who worked in the palace kitchen of a Mogul Emperor. His grandsons now run the place with all the old traditions intact. Even the spelling of korma (qorma) has retained its original Persian form. This dish was cooked for me by Karim's grandson and I enjoyed every morsel with a hot naan. I have deliberately ignored the Mogul Emperors' indulgence in ghee and reduced the quantity drastically.

Soak the saffron in the hot milk and set aside.

In a heavy saucepan, heat the oil over a medium heat and fry the onion for 7–8 minutes until they begin to brown. Add the cashews and continue frying for 6–7 minutes, stirring frequently. Lift them with a slotted spoon and press down with another spoon to drain the excess oil back into the pan. Place the onion and cashews on absorbent paper to cool. Transfer to a blender, add the saffron milk and purée. Set aside.

Add the ghee or butter to the remaining oil in the saucepan. When it has melted, add all the remaining ingredients except the meat and the onion-cashew purée. Cook over a low heat for 2 minutes, then add the meat and the onion-cashew purée. Increase the heat to medium and cook until the mixture begins to bubble.

Reduce the heat to low again, cover the pan with a piece of foil and put the lid on. Seal it by pressing the foil around the rim of the saucepan. Cook for 50-60 minutes, stirring at least twice during cooking. Serve with Jeera Chawal (Cumin flavoured rice), see page 120, and Koshimbir (Raw vegetable salad), see page 143.

Serves 4

a large pinch of saffron strands, pounded

3 tbsp hot milk

3 tbsp sunflower or soya oil

1 large onion, roughly chopped

2 tbsp cashew nuts

2 tbsp ghee or unsalted butter

150 g/5 oz/⅔ cup whole milk plain yogurt, whisked

½–1 tsp chilli powder

4 cloves

6 green cardamom pods, bruised

5 cm/2 in cube root ginger, finely grated

4–5 large cloves garlic, crushed

1½ tbsp ground coriander

1 tsp salt, or to taste

700 g/1½ lb boned leg lamb, trimmed of fat and cut into 5 cm/2 in cubes

My Secret

The royal chefs were as fastidious about choosing the right cuts of meat for their korma as they were about the principles of cooking it. At Karim's I was informed that the least fibrous cuts, such as the neck end of lamb, give better kormas.

Chukander ka Gosht

Lamb with beetroot

Serves 4

2–4 long, slim dried red chillies

4 tbsp sunflower or soya oil

1 large onion, roughly chopped

5 cm/2 in cube root ginger, finely grated

4–5 large cloves garlic, crushed

1½ tbsp ground coriander

700 g/1½ lb boned leg lamb, cut into 2.5 cm/1 in cubes

125 g/4 oz/½ cup whole milk plain yogurt, whisked

2 raw beetroots (beets), peeled and finely grated

1 tsp salt, or to taste

½ tsp garam masala

Beetroot (beet) juice adds a rich colour to this dish. It has great depths of flavour without being spicy.

Soak the chillies in 125 ml/4 fl oz/½ cup of boiling water for 10 minutes.

Meanwhile, heat 2 tablespoons of the oil in a small frying pan over a medium heat and add the onion. Fry for 7–8 minutes until light brown, stirring frequently. Transfer the onion to a blender and add the chillies and their soaking water. Purée until smooth and set aside.

Heat the remaining 2 tablespoons of oil in a heavy saucepan over a low heat and fry the ginger and garlic gently for 1 minute. Add the coriander and fry for 30 seconds.

Increase the heat to medium-high, add the meat and stir-fry for 2–3 minutes. Mix in the whisked yogurt and reduce the heat to low. Cover the pan with a double thickness of foil and put the lid on. Seal the edges by pressing the foil around the rim of the saucepan and cook for 30 minutes.

Meanwhile, place the grated beetroot (beet) in a saucepan and add 300 ml/½ pint/1¼ cups of water. Set over a moderate heat and cook for 15–20 minutes or until tender. Push the beetroot (beet) and its cooking liquid through a sieve to extract as much juice as possible.

Add the beetroot (beet) mixture, onion purée and salt to the meat and stir in 150 ml/¼ pint/⅔ cup of lukewarm water. Cover the pan again with the foil and lid and cook for 15–20 minutes or until the meat is tender.

Stir in the garam masala and remove from the heat. Serve with Jeera Chawal (Cumin flavoured rice), see page 120, or Lasoon ki Roti (Garlic bread), see page 131. Aloo Posto (Potatoes with poppy seeds), see page 36, makes a wonderful side dish.

My Secret
The correct sized pan is essential to cooking a korma successfully. It should hold the meat comfortably; if the pan is too large, the liquid will evaporate faster producing a dry result. Too small a pan will accumulate extra liquid, making the sauce runny.

Gosht ka Shahi Korma

Royal braised lamb

This is an ideal dish for celebration meals or to impress friends. Serve it with Mewa Pulao (Dry fruit pilau), see page 123, and Gajjar-Palak ka Raita (Carrot and spinach in spiced yogurt), see page 139.

Soak the pounded saffron in the hot milk and set aside for 10 minutes.

In a large mixing bowl, whisk the yogurt then add the infused milk, garlic, ginger, mint and lamb. Mix thoroughly, cover the bowl with plastic wrap and refrigerate for 4–5 hours or overnight. Bring the lamb to room temperature before cooking.

In a heavy saucepan, melt the ghee or butter over a low heat and add the cinnamon, cardamom, cloves and bay leaves. Cook gently for 20–25 seconds then add the onion. Increase the heat to medium and fry the onion for 9–10 minutes or until light brown, stirring regularly.

Add the coriander, green chilli, chilli powder and nutmeg. Fry for 1 minute and add the marinated meat and salt. Stir over a medium-high heat for 3–4 minutes. Pour in 125 ml/4 fl oz/½ cup of lukewarm water. Reduce the heat to low and cover the pan with a piece of foil. Place the lid on and seal the pan by pressing the foil round the rim. Cook for 20–25 minutes.

Meanwhile, preheat a small, heavy frying pan or sauté pan over a medium heat. When hot, reduce the heat to low and add the cashews and sunflower seeds. Roast them for about 1 minute, stirring constantly. Add the poppy seeds and stir until the poppy seeds are a shade darker, but not dark brown. Remove from the pan and leave to cool.

In a coffee grinder or spice mill, grind the nut mixture until fine then add it to the meat. Cover the pan with the foil and lid again and cook for a further 20–25 minutes or until the meat is tender. Serve garnished with the toasted almonds.

My Secret
In a classic korma such as this, the water or stock used in cooking is kept to the minimum so that, by the end of the cooking time, it is absorbed back into the meat. The secret of a good korma lies in the prolonged, slow cooking in a properly sealed and very heavy pan.

Serves 6

a large pinch of saffron strands, pounded

2 tbsp hot milk

150 g/5 oz/⅔ cup whole milk plain yogurt

6 large cloves garlic, crushed

5 cm/2 in cube root ginger, finely grated

½ tsp dried mint

1.25 kg/2½ lb boned leg lamb, trimmed of fat and cut into 5 cm/2 in cubes

4 tbsp ghee or unsalted butter

2 x 5 cm/2 in sticks cinnamon

6 green cardamom pods (bruised)

6 cloves

2 bay leaves

1 large onion, finely chopped

1 tbsp ground coriander

1 green chilli, deseeded and finely chopped

½ tsp chilli powder

½ tsp ground nutmeg

1½ tsp salt, or to taste

2 tbsp unroasted cashew nuts, chopped

1 tbsp sunflower seeds

1 tbsp white poppy seeds

toasted flaked almonds, to garnish

Tandoori
Clay oven cooking

The magic of tandoori cooking

A 'tandoor' is a barrel-shaped clay oven that is believed to have found its way into India with the ancient Persians. It must be the most versatile oven in the world, because it is capable of grilling, roasting and baking simultaneously. The cook can, as if by waving a magic wand, produce a variety of dishes at the same time.

Charcoal is used to fuel a tandoor and the food is cooked on a spit. The combination of clay and charcoal produces a fierce heat which seals the outer surface of the meat instantly so that the inside remains moist and succulent during cooking. The food also has an incredibly beautiful, earthy flavour.

You do not have to have a tandoor to cook tandoori food. You can use your oven, grill or barbecue to produce delicious tandoori-style food. If your oven is fitted with a rotisserie, use it in preference to the grill as it will give wonderful results. In good weather, any of the recipes here which require cooking under the grill (broiler) or in an oven can be cooked on the barbecue. However, it will be much easier for you to prepare and cook these if you understand the basic principles.

The tandoor was originally used for making only naan. Gradually, meat and poultry dishes were successfully cooked in the tandoor and, as a result, tandoori food is the most popular among Indian dishes today.

One of the most popular techniques used for cooking meat in the tandoor is known as kabab (kebab). I have combined all the kabab recipes in a separate chapter as some of them are also shallow fried. The meat is prepared in two different ways to produce a variety of kababs. One method is to cut it into small pieces and marinate with spices which are combined with a tenderiser such as plain yogurt, raw papaya purée, or dried and powdered pomegranate seeds. The meat is then skewered and grilled in the tandoor.

In the second method, minced lamb is mixed with herbs and spices and made into desired shapes, then skewered and grilled in the tandoor. You can take it one step further by cooking them on your barbecue. I have included instructions for these too.

The following recipes are exciting and different. They will revolutionise your finger buffets, dinner parties and barbecues, and pamper your palate beyond belief!

Tandoori Kaddu
Tandoori pumpkin

When you bite into a piece of this spicy pumpkin, an explosion of flavours will wake your tastebuds and leave you craving more!
To me, it really is one of the best ways to cook pumpkin or butternut squash. I often eat it with grilled or roasted poultry and find the plain background of the meat extremely satisfying when combined with the spiciness of the vegetable.

Preheat the oven to 200°C/400°F/Gas 6. Quarter the pumpkin or squash, scrape off the seeds and fibres, peel and cut into 2.5 cm/ 1 in cubes.

Place the pumpkin in a bowl and add the oil, garlic, chilli powder, cumin, garam masala and salt. Mix well, then transfer to a baking tray and roast just above the centre of the oven for 20–25 minutes or until the pumpkin is tender and browned.

Arrange on a serving dish and sprinkle the chopped chillies and coriander (cilantro) leaves on top. Serve as an accompaniment to any tandoori dish or kabab.

Serves 4

1 small pumpkin or butternut squash, about 850g/1¾ lb

3 tbsp sunflower or vegetable oil

2–3 large cloves garlic, crushed

½–1 tsp chilli powder

½ tsp ground cumin

½ tsp garam masala

½ tsp salt

1 green chilli, deseeded and finely chopped

1 tbsp coriander (cilantro) leaves, finely chopped

My Secret
For a richer flavour, add melted, unsalted butter instead of the oil (if you do not mind the extra calories!). If you have dried fenugreek leaves in your store cupboard, add 2 teaspoons along with the other ingredients. This lends a rather distinctive flavour to the dish.

Tandoori Phool

Tandoori cauliflower

Serves 4

1 large cauliflower

4 tbsp sunflower or vegetable oil, plus extra for greasing

50 g/2 oz/¼ cup whole milk plain yogurt

2 tbsp double (heavy) cream

1 tbsp besan (gram flour)

2.5 cm/1 in cube root ginger, roughly chopped

3–4 large cloves garlic, roughly chopped

1 tsp ground coriander

½–1 tsp chilli powder

½ tsp ground cumin

½ tsp ground turmeric

1 tsp salt, or to taste

3 tbsp coriander (cilantro) leaves, finely chopped

You can find the best innovative tandoori food in the Bukhara restaurant attached to the luxurious Maurya Sheraton Hotel in New Delhi. That is where I had some wonderful tandoori cauliflower a few years ago. Through plenty of trial and error, I have come up with the following recipe which makes a splendid side dish.

Divide the cauliflower into florets about 3.5 cm/1½ in in diameter. In a large saucepan, bring plenty of salted water to the boil and add the cauliflower. Bring back to the boil and let it cook for precisely 3 minutes. Drain and refresh under cold running water, then plunge the florets into iced water and leave to cool for 30–40 minutes. Drain and place them in a large bowl lined with a clean tea towel to dry thoroughly.

Meanwhile, place 3 tablespoons of the oil and all the remaining ingredients, except the fresh coriander (cilantro), in a blender and process until smooth.

Put the cauliflower in a large, non-metallic mixing bowl and pour the marinade over. Add the coriander leaves and mix thoroughly. Cover and set aside for at least 2 hours.

Preheat the grill (broiler) to high. Remove the rack from the grill-pan and line it with a piece of foil. Brush the foil generously with some oil and arrange the cauliflower florets on it, reserving any remaining marinade. Grill (broil) approximately 12 cm/5 ins below the heat source for 5 minutes.

Mix the leftover marinade with the remaining 1 tablespoon of oil and baste the cauliflower well. Cook for a further 2–3 minutes or until brown spots appear on the florets. Turn them over and cook for another 5 minutes, then baste as above and continue grilling until browned. Remove from the heat and serve.

My Secrets

Be as accurate as possible when determining the size of the cauliflower florets or else they will overcook when blanched.

You can refrigerate the marinating cauliflower overnight if you wish, but it is important to bring it to room temperature before cooking.

Tandoori Aloo

Tandoori potatoes

Tandoori potatoes, cooked in a very hot domestic oven, are so delicious that they can diminish your will-power to zero! They are exciting even when served cold.

In a large saucepan or pot, par-boil the potatoes in plenty of water. Drain, cool slightly then scrape off the skin. Halve each potato lengthways and lay them on a flat surface cut-side down. Make long, deep incisions in them without cutting all the way through. Season with salt and pepper and set aside.

Meanwhile, put the remaining ingredients, except the butter, green chillies and coriander (cilantro) in a blender and process to give a smooth purée. Pour the marinade over the potatoes and mix thoroughly. Cover and leave to marinate for 2 hours.

Preheat the oven to 220°C/425°F/Gas 7. Line a roasting tin with non-stick baking parchment or a piece of foil brushed with oil. Arrange the potatoes on it, spread some of the excess marinade on each piece and reserve the remainder. Bake the potatoes in the centre of the oven for 12–15 minutes. Turn them over and spread with the remaining marinade. Bake for a further 12–15 minutes.

Reserve 2 tablespoons of the melted butter and baste the potatoes with the remainder. Continue to bake for 10–12 minutes or until the potatoes are tender and brown.

Mix the reserved butter with the chilli and coriander and spread it on the potatoes. Bake for another 3–4 minutes, then serve as a side dish with kababs or any tandoori dishes.

Serves 4–6

4 large baking potatoes

50 g/2 oz/¼ cup whole milk plain yogurt

3 tbsp double (heavy) cream

3 tbsp sunflower or vegetable oil, plus extra for greasing

2 tbsp besan (gram flour)

4–5 large cloves garlic, roughly chopped

2.5 cm/1 in cube root ginger, roughly chopped

2 tsp dried fenugreek leaves, stalks removed

1–½ tsp ground cumin

1 tsp ground turmeric

1 tsp salt, or to taste

pepper

½–1 tsp chilli powder

4 tbsp butter, melted

1–2 green chillies, deseeded and finely chopped

2 tbsp coriander (cilantro) leaves, finely chopped

My Secrets

When marinating meat and vegetables, always use a non-metallic container. Glass or ceramic bowls are ideal.

Let the potatoes go cold (or use any leftovers) and cut them into bite-size pieces. Serve on cocktail sticks with drinks.

Tandoori Jhinga

Tandoori king prawns (shrimp)

Serves 4

500 g/1 lb shelled raw king prawns (shrimp)

125 g/4 oz/½ cup plain Greek yogurt

2 tbsp lemon juice

2 tbsp coriander (cilantro) leaves, finely chopped

1 tbsp fresh mint, finely chopped or ½ tsp dried mint

3–4 large cloves garlic, crushed

2.5 cm/1 in cube root ginger, finely grated

1 tbsp besan (gram flour)

1 tsp ground aniseed

1 tsp garam masala

1 tsp salt, or to taste

½–1 tsp chilli powder

½ tsp ground turmeric

4 tbsp sunflower oil

Seafood is at its best in Goa and all along the coastal region of Southern India. Beautiful fresh prawns (shrimp), some of them weighing almost 500 g/1 lb each, are a common sight in this part of the country. I tasted Tandoori Jhinga made from these prawns(shrimp) at a Christmas Eve dinner on a sun-kissed Goan beach a few years ago. The following recipe is recreated based on the memories of this delightful dinner. The prawns (shrimp) are wonderful when barbecued, as they were in Goa.

Devein the prawns (shrimp), wash them gently and pat dry with kitchen paper.

In a bowl, mix the yogurt and all the remaining ingredients, except the oil. Add 2 tablespoons of oil to the marinade and reserve the rest for later. Pour the marinade over the prawns (shrimp) and mix thoroughly. Cover and set aside for 2–3 hours or overnight in the fridge. Leave the prawns (shrimp) at room temperature for about 30 minutes before cooking.

Preheat the grill (broiler) to high for 10 minutes. Brush 4 long metal skewers generously with oil and thread the prawns (shrimp) leaving a gap between each. Mix the remaining oil with any leftover marinade to make a baste. Cook the prawns (shrimp) approximately 12 cm/5 in below the heat source for 5–6 minutes, basting frequently. Alternatively, cook over hot charcoal on the barbecue for 5–6 minutes, basting as above. Serve on a bed of crisp green salad.

My Secret
Besan comes with very tiny lumps. Although it will not affect the taste, it is visually more appealing if the marinade is as smooth as possible. Sprinkle the besan through a sieve over the marinade and mix thoroughly.

Turkey Til Tikka

Grilled turkey breast with sesame seeds

Skinned turkey breast fillets make a delicious alternative to chicken tikka and are readily available in most supermarkets. Sesame seeds add a wonderfully nutty taste and a superb appearance to this dish.

Put the turkey in a mixing bowl. Add the lemon juice and salt and rub well into the meat. Set aside for 20–30 minutes.

Meanwhile, put all the remaining ingredients, except the sesame seeds and oil, into a blender and blend until smooth. Pour the marinade over the turkey and mix well. Cover and refrigerate for 3–4 hours or overnight. Bring the turkey to room temperature before cooking.

Preheat a grill (broiler) to high for 10 minutes. Mix the marinated turkey thoroughly with the sesame seeds. Brush 5–6 metal skewers generously with some of the oil and thread the meat onto them. Grill (broil) approximately 7.5 cm/3 in below the heat source for 4–5 minutes. Mix any leftover marinade with the remaining oil and baste the tikkas frequently. Turn them over and continue cooking for a further 3–4 minutes, basting well. Alternatively, cook over hot charcoal on a barbecue, turning and basting as above. Serve with Tamatar ki Mithi Chutney (Sweet tomato chutney), see page 142.

Serves 4

700 g/1½ lb skinned turkey breast fillets, cut into bite-size pieces

2 tbsp lemon juice

1 tsp salt, or to taste

125 g/4 oz/½ cup plain Greek yogurt

2 tbsp double (heavy) cream

25 g/1 oz/¼ cup mild cheddar cheese, grated

4–5 large cloves garlic, roughly chopped

2.5 cm/1 in cube root ginger, roughly chopped

1 green chilli, deseeded and chopped

1 tbsp besan (gram flour)

1 tsp garam masala

½–1 tsp chilli powder

½ tsp ground turmeric

½ tsp sugar

2 tbsp sesame seeds

4 tbsp sunflower oil

My Secret

To cook the tikkas to perfection, use thick steel skewers as they will conduct the heat efficiently, enabling the meat to cook inside and outside simultaneously. It is also very important to brush the skewers with oil before threading the meat onto them.

Galinha Cafreal

Goan spiced chicken

Serves 4

1 large onion, roughly chopped

6 large cloves garlic, roughly chopped

5 cm/2 in cube root ginger, roughly chopped

1–3 green chillies, deseeded and chopped

2 tbsp lemon juice

2 tsp coriander seeds

1 tsp cumin seeds

½ tsp black peppercorns

seeds of 8 green cardamom pods

2.5 cm/1 in stick cinnamon, broken

4 cloves

4–5 tbsp sunflower or soya oil

1½ tsp salt, or to taste

½ tsp ground turmeric

8 chicken thighs, skinned

4 medium potatoes, about 500 g/1 lb, peeled and halved

4 salad tomatoes, halved

2 tsp desiccated coconut

sprigs of fresh coriander (cilantro), to decorate

Goa, on the West Coast of India and a major tourist attraction today, has a unique cuisine which is a perfect blend of Indian and Portuguese cultures. For this chicken dish, the ingredients are usually prepared in separate pans and combined to give the final dish. This is my simplified version which almost looks after itself in the oven.

Put the onion, garlic, ginger, chillies and lemon juice in a blender and whizz to a smooth purée, adding a little water if necessary. Transfer to a large mixing bowl.

In a coffee grinder or spice mill, grind the coriander, cumin, peppercorns, cardamom, cinnamon and cloves until fine. Add to the spiced onion purée along with the oil, salt and turmeric and mix thoroughly. Add the chicken, mix gently until it is well coated, then cover and set aside for at least 1 hour.

Preheat the oven to 200ºC/400ºF/Gas 6. Put the marinated chicken into a roasting tin, add the potatoes and stir until the potatoes are coated with the spices. Bake in the centre of the oven for 20 minutes. Turn over the chicken and potatoes and bake for a further 15–20 minutes or until browned.

Transfer the chicken and potatoes to a serving dish and arrange the tomatoes around them. Sprinkle the coconut over the tomatoes and garnish with the coriander (cilantro) sprigs.

My Secrets

When making the spiced onion purée, let the blender run for a couple of minutes before deciding whether or not to add water. It may seem difficult at first, but once the onions start releasing their juices, adding water is often not necessary.

Before serving, make sure you scrape every bit of the delicious spice paste from the roasting tin and add it to the chicken and potatoes.

Hariyali Tandoori Murgh

Tandoori chicken with green spice mix

The marinade for green tandoori chicken is rather like Italian pesto minus the pine nuts and using coriander (cilantro) instead of basil. The chicken can be cooked under a hot grill or on the barbecue and makes a very satisfying meal with a raita and a bread such as Andey ki Roti (Bread with spiced eggs), see page 133.

Skin the chicken and make small, deep incisions on both sides of each piece. Put them in a glass bowl or a plastic tub. Sprinkle with the salt and lemon juice and rub them well into the flesh. Set aside for 30 minutes.

In a blender, place the remaining ingredients, except the oil, cumin seeds and vegetables for serving, and process to a smooth paste. Pour this mixture over the chicken and work it well into the flesh. Cover and refrigerate for 4–5 hours or overnight. Bring the chicken back to room temperature before cooking.

Preheat the grill (broiler) to high. Remove the rack from the grill-pan and line with a piece of foil. Brush the foil with a little oil and place the marinated chicken on it, reserving the leftover marinade. Grill (broil) the chicken 12 cm/5 in away from the heat source for 5 minutes. Then turn over and grill for a further 5 minutes.

Reduce the heat to medium and mix the leftover marinade with the oil. Baste the chicken with some of this and continue to grill for 7–8 minutes on each side, basting and turning the chicken over as necessary.

Meanwhile, preheat a small, heavy pan over a medium heat. When hot, reduce the heat to low and dry-roast the cumin for 40–50 seconds, stirring constantly. Remove the cumin from the heat, cool slightly and crush with a pestle or a rolling pin.

When the chicken is ready, remove from the grill and place on a serving dish. Sprinkle the crushed cumin all over the chicken and serve garnished with the bell pepper, red onion and lemon wedges.

Serves 4

4 large chicken quarters, leg or breast

½ tsp salt, or to taste

2 tbsp lemon juice

2 tbsp coriander (cilantro) leaves and stalks, roughly chopped

1–3 green chillies, roughly chopped

5 cm/2 in cube root ginger, roughly chopped

4–5 large cloves garlic, roughly chopped

2 tbsp fresh mint, or 1 tsp dried mint

90 g/3 oz/½ cup whole milk plain yogurt

3 tbsp sunflower or vegetable oil

1 tsp cumin seeds

red bell pepper rings, red onion slices and lemon wedges, to serve

My Secret

The importance of marinating the meat for tandoori cooking cannot be over emphasised. It is in the marinade and the length of time the meat is marinated for, that the secret of successful tandoori cooking lies. The time varies depending on the cut of meat used. For instance, a whole leg or shoulder will take longer than tikka and boti (boneless pieces of chicken and lamb respectively).

Jungli Murgh Mussallam

Tandoori-style whole guinea fowl

Serves 4

For the marinade:

1 guinea fowl, about
1.5 kg/3 lb

juice of ½ lemon

125 g/4 oz/½ cup plain
Greek yogurt

4–5 large cloves garlic,
crushed

2.5 cm/1 in cube root
ginger, finely grated

1 tsp ground coriander

1 tsp ground cumin

1 tsp garam masala

½–1 tsp chilli powder

½ tsp ground turmeric

salt

Guinea fowl is readily available these days as they are now farmed. The full, strong flavour of this bird complements the range of spices that have been used here. When the bird has been stuffed with spicy turkey mince, it makes a much more substantial meal that will be suitable for about four people.

Skin the bird and remove the tips of the wings and legs. Score the breast, legs and thighs with a sharp knife. Rub the lemon juice and 1½ teaspoons of salt all over the bird, making sure that this includes the stomach cavity.

Whisk the yogurt until smooth and add the remaining marinade ingredients. Mix thoroughly and pour the marinade over the guinea fowl. Rub it well into the bird, making sure it penetrates the slits made earlier. Cover and refrigerate for 24 hours. Leave at room temperature for at least 1 hour before cooking.

Meanwhile, to make the stuffing, heat the oil over a medium heat and add the turkey, onion, ginger and garlic. Stir-fry for 3–4 minutes, then add the spices and ½ teaspoon of salt. Continue to stir-fry for a further 3–4 minutes. Add the coriander (cilantro) leaves, remove from the heat and leave to cool.

Preheat the oven to 200°C/400°F/Gas 6. When the stuffing has cooled down, add the beaten egg and mix well. Stuff the stomach cavity of the bird and tie it up with string or secure with trussing needles. Place it on a roasting tin and spread any remaining marinade over the bird.

My Secrets

Skinning poultry is easy if you use a cloth. Hold the bird down with one hand and pull away the skin with the cloth held in the other. Use the same method for joints to prevent slipping. Choose a plain tea cloth without any ridges so that all residues wash off easily. Once you have washed it with detergent and a mild bleach, dry and keep it in a plastic bag ready for next time.

Another key to success for this recipe is to baste the bird frequently to keep it moist.

Roast in the centre of the oven for 20 minutes, then reduce the temperature to 180°C/350°F/Gas 4. Continue roasting for about 40–45 minutes, basting every 10–15 minutes with the melted butter as well as the pan juices.

This recipe is ideally erved with Palak Puri (Deep-fried puffed bread with spinach), see page 130 or Chukandar ki Roti (Beetroot bread), see page 129.

For the stuffing:

2 tbsp sunflower or soya oil

175 g/6 oz minced (ground) turkey

1 small onion, finely chopped

1 cm/½ in cube root ginger, finely grated

2 cloves garlic, crushed

1 tsp ground coriander

½ tsp each of ground cumin, paprika and garam masala

½ tsp ground turmeric

2 tbsp coriander (cilantro) leaves, finely chopped

1 small egg, beaten

2 tbsp butter, melted

Tandoori Chaamp

Tandoori lamb chops

Serves 4

4 lamb chump or shoulder chops, about 700g/1½ lb in total

50 g/2 oz/¼ cup papaya, peeled and chopped (optional)

125 g/4 oz/½ cup whole milk plain yogurt

5 cm/2 in cube root ginger, roughly chopped

5–6 cloves garlic, roughly chopped

1 tsp coriander seeds

1 tsp cumin seeds

2–4 dried red chillies, chopped

2.5 cm/1 in stick cinnamon, broken

seeds of 4 cardamom pods

4 cloves

½ tsp salt

2 tbsp oil, plus extra for greasing

red onion rings, lemon or lime wedges, sliced English cucumber and tomatoes, to serve

In India, green or unripe papaya is puréed and used as a tenderising agent for many meat dishes. The meat used is generally mutton and, although this process is not essential to an ingredient such as lamb, I have found it produces a tender result. In the West, green or unripe papaya tends to be available only in Indian stores but supermarkets often sell papayas that are half-ripe. I tried one of these for this process and was delighted with the result. You do not have to use it, but if you choose to do so, buy a papaya which looks quite green on the outside. Peel it and slice off the very firm flesh from around the surface. The pink flesh deeper inside does not have enough papin (tenderising quality) to be effective, but is delicious.

Remove the rind from the chops and prick both sides of the meat with a fork. Place in a shallow dish in a single layer. Place the papaya (if using), yogurt, ginger and garlic in a blender until smooth.

Grind the coriander, cumin, dried chillies, cinnamon, cardamom and cloves in a coffee grinder or spice mill until fine. Stir into the yogurt mixture with the salt and pour the marinade over the chops. Using a fork, mix them thoroughly, lifting and turning to make sure that both sides of the meat are coated with the marinade. Cover and refrigerate for 4–6 hours or overnight. Bring the meat to room temperature before cooking.

Preheat a grill (broiler) to high. Remove the rack from the grill-pan and line it with foil. Brush the foil with a little oil and place the chops on it. Mix the leftover marinade with the oil. Grill (broil) the chops about 12 cm/5 in below the heat source for 5 minutes. Turn over and grill for a further 5 minutes, then baste generously with the marinade. Continue cooking for 3–4 minutes and turn them over again. Brush with the remaining marinade and grill for a final 3–4 minutes. Serve garnished with the red onion, lemon or lime, English cucumber and tomatoes.

My Secret

Cook these chops on the barbecue and enjoy the spice-infused smoky flavour. I add the oil when marinating the chops if I want to cook them on the barbecue. Wherever you cook them, the key to a succulent, juicy result is to baste the meat frequently and generously. Frequent basting will give a light crust on the surface and keep the meat beautifully moist inside.

Assado de Leitoa
Goan spicy roast pork

This spicy offering comes from Goa, popularly known as the Pearl of the Orient. As well as a sublime natural beauty spot that attracts thousands of tourists every year, Goa is also well known for its unique cuisine which evolved with the Portuguese during their colonisation of the area.

Remove the trussing and the crackling from the joint. Score the pork on all sides with a sharp knife. Rub in the vinegar followed by the salt and set aside for 30 minutes.

Meanwhile, place the cumin, peppercorns, cinnamon, dried chillies and cloves in a coffee grinder or spice mill and grind until fine. Transfer to a mixing bowl and add the garlic, ginger and turmeric. Add 3–4 tablespoons of water to make a thick paste and rub it well into the pork. Cover and refrigerate overnight. Bring it back to room temperature before cooking.

Preheat the oven to 200°C/400°F/Gas 6. Place the marinated pork in a roasting tin and roast just above the centre of the oven for 20 minutes. Reduce the temperature to 190°C/375°F/Gas 5. Spoon half the wine over the joint and cook for 15 minutes. Turn it over, spoon on the remaining wine and cook for 35–40 minutes, basting frequently with the pan juices. Transfer the pork to a lower shelf for the last 10–15 minutes.

Remove the joint from the oven and let it cool. When it is cool enough to handle, slice the meat into thick strips.

In a frying pan or sauté pan, heat the oil over a medium heat and fry the onion for 9–10 minutes until light brown, stirring frequently. Add the sliced meat and fresh chillies and fry for 6–8 minutes until well browned.

Add 150 ml/5 fl oz/⅔ cup of boiling water to the roasting tin and scrape off all the caramelized pan juices. Strain the juice into the meat, cook for 1–2 minutes, then remove from the heat.

Serves 4–5

1 kg/2¼ lb boneless leg of pork

3 tbsp white wine or cider vinegar

1½ tsp salt, or to taste

1½ tsp cumin seeds

1 tsp black peppercorns

5 cm/2 in stick cinnamon, broken

1–3 dried red chillies, chopped

6 cloves

1 bulb garlic (12–14 cloves), crushed

5 cm/2 in cube root ginger, finely grated

1 tsp ground turmeric

1 glass dry white wine

4 tbsp sunflower or vegetable oil

1 large onion, finely sliced

1–2 green chillies, deseeded and cut into strips

My Secrets
The meat has to be of prime quality. Marinating for several hours is essential and, to allow the flavours to penetrate deep inside, the meat has to be skinned and the flesh scored before marinating.

Serve with Lasoon ki Roti (Garlic bread), see page 131, Chukander ki Roti (Beetroot bread), see page 129, or a vegetable dish such as Dum ki Subzi (Spiced steamed vegetables), see page 49.

Kabab

Kebab

The classic kabab

Kababs found their way into India from Turkey and Central Asia, where they are known as kebabs. Now one of the favourite ways of preparing meat, kababs can be made of minced (ground) meat, or chunks of meat cut into small pieces, or flattened and cut into strips. The most popular kababs such as shami, tikka and seekh were originally nomadic inventions; the nomads simply cooked the meat from the day's hunt by hanging it over a wood fire.

Today's delicious kababs have evolved over centuries and reached gourmet status through the skill and imagination of Indian chefs. Numerous varieties are available, from small chunks of meat marinated in fragrant spiced yogurt to pastes of meat laced with herbs and spices.

Kababs that are traditionally cooked in a tandoor are also ideal for barbecuing (chargrilling). I find the aroma of the spices wafting through the hot charcoal smoke totally irresistible. There are other recipes that fill the air with an alluring aroma when shallow or deep fried. Whichever variety you make, you will find kababs are the kind of food that diminishes your will-power to zero!

Paneer Pasanda

Marinated pan-fried strips of Indian cheese

The word pasanda is often misunderstood in the West. It is commonly believed to be the sauce in which the meat is cooked but in fact pasanda is a specific style of cutting meat in a fashion similar to goujon or schnitzel. It can be cooked with or without a sauce. If using halloumi instead of Indian paneer cheese for this recipe, remember to adjust the level of salt to taste.

Cut the cheese into strips measuring 5 cm x 5 mm/2 x ½ in. If using paneer, bring a pan full of water to the boil and add the strips. Bring back to the boil and cook for 3–4 minutes, then drain. Leave to cool for a few minutes.

Cut the bell pepper and the onion to match the strips of cheese and put them all in a mixing bowl.

Put the remaining ingredients, except the oil, butter and royal cumin or caraway seeds, in a blender and process to give a smooth purée. Pour the marinade over the cheese and vegetables and mix thoroughly. Cover and leave to marinate for 1–2 hours.

In a large, non-stick sauté or frying pan, heat the oil and butter together over a medium-high heat. Add the royal cumin or caraway seeds and fry for 15–20 seconds, then add the marinated ingredients. Increase the heat to high and fry for 4–5 minutes, stirring frequently.

Reduce the heat to medium and fry, stirring well, for a further 3–4 minutes or until browned. Remove from the heat and serve with any bread.

Serves 4

225g/8 oz/1cup block paneer or halloumi cheese

1 large red bell pepper, about 250g/9oz

1 large red onion

3 tbsp double (heavy) cream

1 tbsp whole milk plain yogurt

2–3 large cloves garlic, roughly chopped

1 cm/½ in cube root ginger, roughly chopped

½–1 tsp chilli powder

1 tsp ground coriander

½ tsp ground cumin

½ tsp ground turmeric

2 tsp dried fenugreek leaves, stalks removed

½ tsp salt

2 tbsp sunflower or vegetable oil

1 tbsp butter

½ tsp royal cumin (shahi jeera) or caraway seeds

My Secrets

Boiling the cheese before marinating allows it to absorb all of the flavours.

It is important to use a large frying pan for quick evaporation of the moisture content. If you do not have one, cook this in batches, keeping the cooked strips in a hot oven, without a cover.

Nariyal ke Kabab

Coconut kebabs

Makes 16

150 g/5 oz/½ cup
desiccated coconut

150 ml/5 fl oz/½ cup hot
milk

2 large slices white bread,
crusts removed

90 g/3½ oz/¼ cup besan
(gram flour)

1–3 green chillies, roughly
chopped

2.5 cm/1 in cube root
ginger, roughly chopped

1 large clove garlic,
roughly chopped

2 tbsp coriander (cilantro)
leaves and stalks, roughly
chopped

½ tsp chilli powder
(optional)

½ tsp salt, or to taste

1 medium onion, finely
chopped

oil, for shallow frying

*The very sight of coconut conjures up images of religious occasions
in India. In Hindu mythology, coconut is regarded as the fruit of the
gods. For every religious event coconut is placed in a prominent
place on a full pot of rice. This is supposed to auger well for a life full
of rich experiences.*

Put the coconut in a mixing bowl, pour over the hot milk and set
aside for 10 minutes.

Cut the bread into small pieces and place it in a food processor.
Add the soaked coconut and milk, plus all the remaining ingredients,
except the onion and oil. Blend to a smooth paste, then stir in the
chopped onion by hand. Divide the mixture into 16 balls about the
size of a lime and flatten them into smooth, round cakes. If the
mixture sticks while shaping, dip your fingers in cold water.

Pour enough oil into a frying pan to give a depth of about 1 cm/½ in
and set over a high heat. Working in batches, fry the kababs until
brown on both sides. Drain on absorbent paper and serve
accompanied by Aam ki Chutney (Mango dip), see page 145, with
drinks, or with Tamatar ki Mithi Chutney (Sweet tomato chutney), see
page 142, as a first course.

My Secrets

In India, these delicious little morsels are made of freshly grated
coconut. Do try them with fresh coconut if you have the time, but
desiccated coconut moistened with a little milk is a good alternative.

Don't overcrowd the pan when frying the kababs so that they are
cooked evenly through.

Shakahari Tikka Kabab

Vegetarian flat cakes

For these delicious vegetarian kebabs, you can use either minced (ground) Quorn or minced (ground) soya. If you use soya mince, you will need 125 g/4 oz. Soak it in 225 ml/8 fl oz/1 cup hot water, which will be absorbed by the soya in a few minutes. You can then proceed with the recipe the same way as for using Quorn mince below.

Heat the sunflower oil over a medium heat, then fry the onion, chillies and ginger for 5–6 minutes until soft.

In a mixing bowl, combine the remaining ingredients, except for the oil. Add the fried ingredients and mix well. Divide the mixture into two equal parts and make 6 equal-sized balls out of each. Flatten each one into a round cake, about 5 mm/¼ in thick.

In a frying pan, heat the oil for shallow-frying over a medium heat. When hot, fry the kababs in batches until golden brown on both sides. Remove and drain on kitchen paper (paper towels).

Serve with chutney as a starter or side dish.

Makes 12

2 tbsp sunflower oil

1 large onion, finely chopped

2 fresh green chillies, deseeded and finely chopped

2.5 cm/1 in cube root ginger, finely grated

225 g/8 oz/2 cups minced (ground) Quorn

2 tsp ground coriander

½ tsp garam masala

2 tbsp coriander (cilantro) leaves, chopped

1 tsp salt, or to taste

25 g/1 oz/⅓ cup cornmeal (maize)

25 g/1 oz/⅓ cup cornflour (corn starch)

2 large (extra-large) eggs, beaten

oil, for shallow-frying

My Secret

For enhanced taste and a contrast in texture, add 1 tablespoon finely chopped cashews or almonds to the mixture. If you have a nut allergy, try crushed sunflower seeds instead. These will also provide plenty of dietary fibre.

Gulnaar Kabab

Chicken kebabs in a rich red sauce

Serves 4

4 chicken breast fillets, skinned, about 700 g/1½ lb in total

150 ml/5 fl oz/½ cup milk

6 green cardamom pods, bruised

5 cm/2 in stick cinnamon

2 tbsp white poppy seeds

4–5 tbsp sunflower or vegetable oil

1 large onion, roughly chopped

5 cm/2 in cube root ginger, roughly chopped

5–6 cloves garlic, roughly chopped

2 tbsp unsalted cashew nuts, chopped

150 ml/5 fl oz/½ cup double (heavy) cream

½–1 tsp chilli powder

1 tsp salt, or to taste

2 tbsp tomato purée (paste)

a few unsprayed red rose petals, washed

When I was in Lucknow, in Northern India, recently, gulnaar kababs made a lasting impression on me. It was an exotic, evocative and totally alluring dish containing succulent chunks of chicken in a thick, rich red sauce surrounded by equally rich red rose petals.

Put the chicken fillets in a large plastic bag and flatten them slightly with a meat mallet. Remove and cut each fillet into 2 pieces. Place them in a saucepan with the milk, cardamom pods and cinnamon. Place over a medium heat and stir until the chicken turns opaque. Cover the pan and reduce the heat to low and cook for 15 minutes. Meanwhile, grind the poppy seeds in a coffee or spice mill until fine.

Using tongs, transfer the cooked chicken pieces to a plate. Strain the cooking juices and set them aside – you should have about 150 ml/ 5 fl oz/⅔ cup, if not add a little water to make up the difference.

Heat 2 tablespoons of the oil in a small saucepan over a medium heat and fry the onion for 3–4 minutes. Add the ginger, garlic and cashews and continue cooking, stirring, until the ingredients are light brown. Remove from the heat and let cool for a few minutes, then purée the mixture in a blender with the cream. Set aside.

Heat the remaining oil in a sauté or frying pan over a low heat and add the ground poppy seeds. Fry for 1 minute, then add the chilli powder and salt and continue frying for 30 seconds. Add the tomato purée, cook for 1 minute, then add the onion purée and cook gently for 4–5 minutes, stirring constantly.

Add the chicken and the strained cooking juices to the pan. Cook, uncovered, for 4–5 minutes or until the sauce is reduced to the consistency of a thick paste and clings to the pieces of chicken. Remove from the heat, garnish with the rose petals and serve with a roti and a vegetable dish or raita.

My Secret
The word 'Gulnaar' refers to the richness of the red that is similar to the colour of pomegranate seeds. In this case, it is the rich red rose petals on which the name of the dish is based. Moghul Emperor Babur was noted for his love of roses, which are represented in the dish through the red of the chilli seeds. To create a similar effect without the hotness, use kasmir chilli powder or paprika.

Tangri Kabab
Marinated chicken drumsticks

The combination of charcoal and spice produces unmatched aroma and taste. This is probably the reason why tandoori food is popular. The word tangri is derived from the Hindi word meaning the lower leg.

Make 2–3 small, deep slits on each drumstick. Sprinkle with the lemon juice and salt and rub them well into the chicken. Set aside.

In a large bowl, mix together the remaining ingredients except the cumin, dried mint and butter, until well blended. Add the chicken and mix until all the pieces are well coated. Cover and set aside for 2–3 hours, or marinate overnight in the fridge, bringing the chicken back to room temperature before cooking.

In a small heavy pan, dry-roast the cumin seeds over a medium-low heat for about 1 minute. Cool and crush them with the back of a wooden spoon or a rolling pin.

Preheat an overhead grill (broiler) to high. Remove the grid from the grill pan and line it with foil. Brush the foil lightly with melted butter and arrange the drumsticks on it. Spoon any remaining marinade equally over the drumsticks. Grill (broil) for 5 minutes, setting the chicken about 7.5 cm/3 in below the heat source. Turn the drumsticks over and grill for a further 2–3 minutes, then baste them with some of the melted butter. Sprinkle half the mint over the drumstick and continue to grill for 2–3 minutes.

Turn them over again and baste with the remaining butter as well as the pan juices. Sprinkle the remaining mint over and grill (broil) for a further 3–4 minutes. Remove from the grill and sprinkle with the roasted cumin immediately, then serve.

Serves 4

8 chicken drumsticks, skinned

1½ tbsp lemon juice

1 tsp salt, or to taste

125 g/4 oz/½ cup plain Greek yogurt

5 cm/2 in cube root ginger, finely grated

4–5 large cloves garlic, crushed

½–1 tsp chilli powder

½ tsp ground turmeric

1 tsp cumin seeds

½ tsp dried mint

2 tbsp butter, melted

My Secrets
Strained yogurt is best for marinating tandoori dishes to give them the characteristic dry surface with succulent and moist interior.

Melted butter is not necessary when the drumsticks are barbecued, but you could brush a little on before removing them from the rack.

The drumsticks can also be cooked on an open barbecue but will take a few minutes longer.

The food in the tandoor (Indian clay oven) is cooked with a lid on and you can easily replicate this at home with a barbecue that has a lid.

Chapli Kabab

Minced lamb or beef kebab

Makes 8

1 large egg

1 large slice white bread, crusts removed

2 tbsp milk

2 large cloves garlic, roughly chopped

1–2 green chillies

1 tsp garam masala

1 tsp salt, or to taste

15 g/½ oz/¾ cup coriander (cilantro) leaves and stalks, roughly chopped

2 tbsp fresh mint, or 1 tsp dried mint

500 g/1 lb/2 cups lean minced (ground) lamb or beef

½ small onion, roughly chopped

oil for brushing

These kababs are rather like burgers but much thinner. They can be served in numerous ways – one of my favourites is to serve them in a pita pocket with a little salad and my Pudina-dhaniya ka Chawal (Mint and coriander rice), see page 122. They also make a very satisfying meal when served with boiled basmati rice, Dhal Panch-phoron (Red lentils with five-spice seasoning), see page 19, and a raita. You could also treat yourself to an Indian-style hamburger and Tamatar ki Mithi Chutney (Sweet tomato chutney), see page 142!

In a food processor, blend the egg, bread and milk until smooth. Add all the remaining ingredients except the onion and oil. Blend until all the ingredients are well incorporated and the mixture is smooth. Add the onion and blend again using the pulse action so that the onion is finely chopped rather than puréed. Divide the mixture into 8 equal portions and flatten them out to about 10 cm/4 in in diameter.

Brush the kababs with a little oil and cook over a moderately hot barbecue, char-grill or griddle for 2 minutes on each side; alternatively cook under a preheated grill or broiler for 2½ minutes on each side, setting the kababs 7.5 cm/3 in away from the heat source.

My Secrets

I like to add milk to the kabab mixture because the lactic acid in it makes the kababs deliciously tender. For an extra-special treat, try adding single (light) cream instead of the milk; the kababs will simply melt in your mouth!

You will find it easier to shape the kababs if you have a bowl of cold water ready to moisten your palms each time.

Nargisi Kabab

Hard boiled eggs encased in spiced lamb

You may think of this simply as an 'Indian-style Scotch Egg', but a lot of tender thoughts went into its creation during the Mogul rule in India. The name was inspired by a tribute from a famous Mogul poet to the beautiful narcissus-like eyes of a woman (the Urdu name for the narcissus flower is nargis). The cooked kabab is halved lengthways to resemble the eye and reveals the contrast of the pale brown meat mixture, the white of the egg and the golden yolk.

In a sauté or small frying pan, heat the oil over medium heat and fry the onion, garlic and ginger for 5–6 minutes or until browned.

Cut the bread into small pieces and place it in a food processor with the yogurt and one of the raw eggs and blend to a paste. Add the fried onion mixture, meat, fresh coriander (cilantro), mint, garam masala, chilli powder and salt. Blend until the mixture is smooth, then divide it into 6 equal portions.

Shell the hard-boiled eggs and wrap each one in a piece of the meat mixture, taking care to enclose it completely and following the egg shape carefully. In a small bowl, blend the cornflour (cornstarch) with a little water and beat it with the remaining raw egg.

Heat the oil over a medium heat in a wok, deep-fryer or large heavy saucepan. When the oil has a faint shimmer on the surface, dip each kabab in the egg and cornflour mixture and use your fingers to rub it all over several times to ensure that the kabab is well protected. Fry 2–3 kababs at a time for 10–12 minutes, turning them frequently, until well browned. Drain on absorbent paper.

Halve the kababs and serve surrounded by the lemon, tomatoes, onion and lettuce. They are ideal for a buffet party, picnic or as a main meal when served with bread and a lentil dish.

My Secrets

Traditionally, besan (gram flour) is roasted and used to bind the meat mixture, and the kababs are simmered in a spicy tomato sauce. The entire dish is known as Nargisi Kofta, but I like them without the sauce and find it easier to use bread and egg to bind the meat. As they are not smothered in sauce, they can easily qualify as kababs.

Woks are ideal for deep-frying and their shape allows you to use less oil than other pans.

I find it easier to halve the cooked kababs using a serrated knife.

Makes 6

2 tbsp sunflower or soya oil

1 large onion, chopped

4–5 large cloves garlic, roughly chopped

5 cm/2 in cube ginger root, roughly chopped

2 large slices white bread, crusts removed

2 tbsp plain yogurt

2 large raw eggs, plus 6 hard-boiled eggs

500 g/1 lb/2 cups lean minced (ground) lamb or beef

2 tbsp coriander (cilantro) leaves and stalks

2–3 tbsp fresh mint, or 1 tsp dried mint

1½ tsp garam masala

1 tsp chilli powder

1 tsp salt, or to taste

2 tbsp cornflour (cornstarch)

oil, for deep-frying

lemon wedges, tomato wedges, sliced red onions and shredded iceberg lettuce, to garnish

Shami Kabab

Spiced minced lamb patties

500 g/1 lb/2 cups lean minced (ground) lamb or beef

125 g/4 oz/½ cup channa dhal or yellow split peas

2 tbsp sunflower or soya oil

1 medium onion, roughly chopped

5 cm/2 in cube root ginger, roughly chopped

4 large cloves garlic, roughly chopped

2 long, slim dried red chillies, chopped

2.5cm/1 in stick cinnamon, broken

seeds of 6 green cardamom pods

4 cloves

½ tsp black peppercorns

1 tsp cumin seeds

2 tsp white poppy seeds

1 tsp salt, or to taste

1 tbsp lemon juice

2–3 tbsp fresh mint, or 1 tsp dried mint

2 tbsp cup coriander (cilantro) leaves and stalks

2 large eggs

1½ tbsp cornflour (cornstarch)

oil, for shallow frying

These beautifully fragrant kababs are made with minced (ground) lamb, or beef, mixed with channa dhal, which are sold by Indian stores and health food shops. You can use yellow split peas instead but they do not have the distinctive nutty flavour of channa dhal.

Put the minced (ground) meat and the dahl or split peas in a large saucepan and add 300 ml/½ pint/1¼ cups water. Bring to the boil, then reduce the heat to medium and cook, uncovered, for 10–12 minutes. Reduce the heat slightly and continue simmering for about 10 minutes or until the pulses are tender but not mushy. Increase the heat, if necessary, and cook for a few minutes longer to ensure the mixture is dry. If the meat you are using is not very lean, then drain off the fat at this stage.

While the meat and the lentils are cooking, heat the oil in a frying pan over a medium heat and fry the onion, ginger, garlic and red chilli for 5–6 minutes until browned. In a coffee grinder or spice mill, grind the cinnamon, cardamom seeds, cloves, peppercorns, cumin and poppy seeds until fine. Transfer to a food processor and add the fried onion mixture, cooked meat and lentils, lemon juice, mint, coriander (cilantro), one of the eggs and the salt. Process until the ingredients are well blended.

Divide the meat mixture into 16 equal sized portions and, with wet hands, shape each into a miniature cup shape. In a mixing bowl, combine all the ingredients for the stuffing and fill the meat cups with a little of the mixture, enclosing it completely with the meat. Flatten each kabab slightly to form a 2.5cm/1 in thick cake.

My Secrets

It is a good idea to divide the stuffing into 16 equal portions before you start filling the meat cups.

More often than not, when I have to cook against the clock, tradition does pale into insignificance! I omit the stuffing but add the green chilli and coriander leaves to the meat mixture.

It is useful to have a spice mill or coffee grinder dedicated to spices. You could use a mortar and pestle to grind spices, seeds and nuts finely, but it will be hard work.

In a small bowl, blend the cornflour (cornstarch) with a little water and beat in the second egg. Pour enough oil into a frying pan to measure about 1 cm/½ in deep and heat over a medium-high heat. Dip each kabab in the egg mixture making sure it is generously coated, then fry until well browned, 2–3 minutes on each side. Drain on absorbent paper. Serve as a starter with Lasoon Ki Roti (Garlic bread) see page 131, cut into triangles and a chutney or raita, or as a main course with a vegetable curry and bread or rice.

For the stuffing:

1 small onion, very finely chopped

1 green chilli, deseeded and finely chopped

2 tbsp coriander (cilantro) leaves, finely chopped

1 small tomato, deseeded and finely chopped

Peshawari Kabab
Peshawar-style skewered lamb

Serves 4

700 g/1½ lb boned leg lamb, cut into 2.5cm/1 in cubes

125 g/4 oz/½ cup whole milk plain yogurt, or Greek yogurt

2 tbsp light malt vinegar

5 cm/2 in cube root ginger, roughly chopped

5–6 large cloves garlic, roughly chopped

1 small onion, roughly chopped

1–2 green chillies, chopped

1 tbsp fresh mint, or 1 tsp dried mint

2–3 tbsp coriander (cilantro) leaves and stalks, chopped

1 tsp ground cumin

1 tsp garam masala

1 tsp salt

oil for greasing

4 tbsp butter, melted

These delicious lamb kababs originated in Peshawar, in the mountainous region of the North West Frontier Province (NWFP), in Pakistan. This area is noted for its rugged beauty as well as being a mountaineer's paradise. When I was in boarding school in mountainous North East India, I envied my cousin, a day pupil, who was sent lunch from home: it would often consist of hot Peshawari Kababs wrapped in delicious toasted chapatties, and I had to be content with my 'school dinner'! Now I make them for a quick lunch or for the picnic basket. Sometimes I even use bought soft flour tortillas instead of chapatties.

Put the meat in a large mixing bowl. Purée all the remaining ingredients, except the oil and butter, in a food processor and pour the mixture over the meat. Mix well, then cover the bowl and refrigerate for 4–5 hours or overnight. Bring the lamb to room temperature before cooking.

Preheat a grill (broiler) to high. Remove the grid from the grill-pan and line it with a piece of foil, then brush with oil. Thread the marinated cubes of lamb onto lightly oiled skewers leaving a slight gap between each piece of meat.

Place the skewered meat on the prepared grill-pan and cook approximately 7.5 cm/3 in below the heat source for 5 minutes. Brush the kababs generously with half the melted butter and continue cooking for 2–3 minutes. Turn them over, cook for 5 minutes, then brush with the remaining butter. Continue to cook for 1–2 minutes, remove from the heat and serve hot or cold with Jeera Chawal (Cumin flavoured rice), see page 120, and Subzion ka Korma (Vegetable korma), see page 67.

My Secrets
You can safely leave the lamb marinating in the fridge for up to 48 hours.

If you have a ridged cast iron griddle, use this for cooking the kebabs. Pre-heat the griddle, lightly brushed with oil for at least 3–4 minutes. use short bamboo skewers oiled as above. The flavour imparted by this method of cooking is deliciously different.

Kaleji Pasanda Kabab

Marinated lamb's liver

Strips of lamb's liver marinated in spicy yogurt and cooked under a hot grill makes a superb wholesome dish. You can serve it as a starter with salad or as a main course with a raita and bread. You will need 6–8 skewers to make this dish.

Remove any membrane and gristle from the liver and wash gently. Dry thoroughly with absorbent paper and cut into thin strips about 5 cm/2 in long.

Put the yogurt, onion, garlic, ginger, lemon juice, cumin, chilli powder and salt in a blender and process to a smooth purée. Place the liver in a mixing bowl and pour the marinade over. Mix thoroughly, then cover the bowl and refrigerate for 4–5 hours or overnight. Bring the liver back to room temperature before cooking.

Preheat the grill (broiler) to high for about 10 minutes. Oil the skewers and thread the strips of liver onto them. Grill (broil) approximately 7.5 cm/3 in below the heat source for 5–6 minutes, basting with the oil and turning the kababs over halfway through cooking. Serve with the lettuce, red onions, lemon and chillies or bell pepper.

Serves 4–5

700 g/1½ lb lamb's liver

125 g/4 oz/½ cup plain Greek yogurt

½ small onion, roughly chopped

4–5 large cloves garlic, roughly chopped

2.5 cm/1 in cube root ginger, roughly chopped

1 tbsp lemon juice

1½ tsp ground cumin

½–1 tsp chilli powder

1 tsp salt, or to taste

3 tbsp sunflower or soya oil

shredded lettuce, sliced red onions, lemon wedges, strips of fresh red chillies or bell pepper, to serve

My Secrets

Dressing up leftovers is as important as cooking well. If you have any of these superb pasanda kababs left, try a delicious Liver Pilau. Halve the strips of cooked liver and cook Mewa Pulao (page 123) and as soon as the pulao is ready, pile the liver on top of the rice, put the lid on and let it heat through for 10 minutes, then serve. The new dish will delight you with the most wonderful contrast in taste and texture.

To make a colourful presentation, use a few strips of green and red pepper in each skewer. Baste them well when you baste the liver.

Talana

Deep-frying

Pampering the palette with snacks

Innumerable varieties of dishes are produced by deep-frying. In India, a karahi, a heavy cast-iron pan shaped like a wok, is generally used and its shape means you do not need to use a huge quantity of oil. This avoids the need to strain and store the oil for reuse over a long period of time; it is quite easy to use it up in general cooking because you only have a small amount left.

A few simple rules will produce light and crisp deep-fried food which will also have a clean taste. First of all, choose a light cooking oil. I like sunflower oil best. Secondly, make sure the oil is at the right temperature. If you have a thermometer, check that the oil is around 180°C/350°F. A good way to judge the temperature without a thermometer is to ensure that the surface of the oil has a faint shimmer of rising smoke. You could also drop a tiny piece of bread into the hot oil: it should rise to the surface in a few seconds without browning and the browning should take a minute or longer.

Vegetables, meat, fish and so on are coated in a spicy batter and deep-fried to produce mouth-watering snacks. They are rather like Japanese tempura, but instead of plain flour, the Indian version uses besan or gram flour, which is made from chickpeas (garbanzos). These snacks are great at drinks parties or buffet meals. I don't know of anyone who does not enjoy these wonderfully crisp finger foods – even if they are health-food fanatics, they weaken at the sight of these delicious morsels! Some of these finger foods and snacks are also shallow fried.

Makki ke Pakore

Baby corn fritters

I have used baby sweetcorn to create this sensational snack, though it is not commonly used in India. The mature corn, on the other hand, can be used freely to cook a variety of dishes ranging from snacks to main meals.

Mix all the dry ingredients together in a bowl. Gradually add 200 ml/ 7 fl oz/¾ cup of water to form a thick paste of coating consistency.

In a wok or other pan suitable for deep-frying, heat the oil over a medium heat. When the surface of the oil has a faint shimmer of rising smoke, dip each piece of baby sweetcorn into the batter and shake off any excess.

Working in batches so you don't overcrowd the pan, fry the baby sweetcorn in a single layer for 7–8 minutes or until they are crisp and golden brown. Drain on absorbent paper and serve with a relish if you wish, though they are tasty enough without one.

Serves 6–8

110 g/4 oz/¾ cup besan (gram flour)

50 g/2 oz/¼ cup cornmeal

2 tsp ground coriander

2 tsp ground cumin

1 tsp crushed dried red chillies or chilli powder

1 tsp onion seeds

1 tsp salt, or to taste

½ tsp aniseed

½ tsp ground turmeric

a very small pinch of bicarbonate of soda

sunflower or soya oil, for deep-frying

225 g/8 oz/1 cup whole baby sweetcorn

My Secret
Aniseed is used in order to make deep-fried food easily digestible. If you do not have aniseed, use ¼ teaspoon ground asafoetida, which also helps digestion.

Masalewale Badam aur Kaju

Spiced almonds and cashews

Serves 8-10

150 g/5 oz/½ cup shelled almonds

150 g/5 oz/½ cup raw cashew nuts

2 tsp ground coriander

1 tsp ground cumin

½–1 tsp chilli powder

½ tsp garlic powder

25 g/1 oz/¼ cup besan (gram flour), sieved

oil, for deep-frying

A drinks party is not complete without a few fried or roasted nuts. Who can resist the temptation? They are even more irresistible when coated with a touch of spice. If you choose them carefully and prepare them with an imaginative twist, they will have your guests joyously murmuring with curiosity and admiration.

Put the nuts in a mixing bowl and add the remaining ingredients except the besan (gram flour) and oil. Mix in 4 tablespoons of water, stirring until thoroughly combined, then add the besan and stir until the nuts are evenly coated.

Heat the oil in a wok or other pan suitable for deep-frying over a medium heat. When hot but not smoking, add the nuts (working in batches if necessary) and fry them for 6–8 minutes or until they begin to crackle gently. Drain on absorbent paper.

Allow to cool thoroughly before storing in an airtight jar. They will keep well for a couple of weeks.

My Secret
I like to add 125 g/4 oz/¾ cup dry roasted peanuts to the mixutre to add extra texture and depth to the flavour. Mix into the homemade nut mixture while it is still hot.

Aloo ke Pakore

Spicy potato fritters

Pakoras made from all kinds of vegetables are very popular all over India. These pakoras are delicious served as a side dish or as delightful morsels to go with drinks. In India, we often have them with afternoon tea instead of cakes and biscuits.

Cut the peeled potatoes into small pieces. In a large saucepan, boil them in plenty of salted water until tender but not mushy. Leave to drain and dry in a colander, then mash lightly with a fork.

In a small saucepan, heat 2 tablespoons of the oil over a medium heat and add the cumin seeds. As soon as they splutter, add the onion, green chilli and ginger. Fry for 3–4 minutes until the onion is soft. Stir in the coriander (cilantro) leaves, salt and turmeric, then remove from the heat.

Add the mashed potatoes, then the cornflour (cornstarch) and beaten egg. Stir until all the ingredients are well blended.

In a wok or other suitable pan, heat some oil for deep-frying over a medium-high heat. Drop a tiny amount of the potato mixture into the oil to test the temperature – if it starts sizzling and floating to the top immediately, the oil is at the right temperature.

Pick up 1 tablespoon of the potato mixture and, with another spoon, make a rough croquette shape, then gently push it into the hot oil. Fry as many as the pan will hold in a single layer without overcrowding the pan. Cook for 5–6 minutes or until well browned then drain on absorbent paper.

Serves 4

500 g/1 lb potatoes, peeled

sunflower or vegetable oil, for frying

½ tsp cumin seeds

1 medium onion, finely chopped

1 green chilli, finely chopped

2.5 cm/1 in cube root ginger, finely grated

2 tbsp coriander (cilantro) leaves, finely chopped

1 tsp salt, or to taste

½ tsp ground turmeric

2 tbsp cornflour (cornstarch)

1 large egg, beaten

My Secret
One of the golden rules of crisp and dry deep-fried food is not to overcrowd the pan. This causes the temperature of the oil to drop and will give a soggy result. It can also cause food such as these pakoras to break up.

Simla Mirch ke Pakore

Batter-fried sweet pepper rings

Serves 4–6

2 large green bell peppers

2 large red bell peppers

125 g/4 oz/¾ cup besan (gram flour)

2 tbsp ground rice

1½ tsp ground cumin

1 tsp aniseed

½–1 tsp chilli powder

½ tsp ground turmeric

½ tsp salt

sunflower oil, for deep-frying

You will need the will-power of a saint to resist these sweet and juicy bell peppers, coated in a lightly spiced batter and deep-fried until they have become crisp!

Slice off the top and tail of the bell peppers and cut them into 1 cm/½ in rings. Scrape off the white pith and discard the seeds.

Mix the remaining ingredients, except the oil, in a mixing bowl and gradually add 175 ml/6 fl oz/¾ cup of water. Stir until a thick batter is formed.

Heat the oil over a medium-high heat in a karahi, wok or other pan suitable for deep-frying. When the oil has a faint shimmer of rising smoke, dip each bell pepper ring in the batter and fry, without overcrowding the pan, for 3–4 minutes or until they are crisp and golden brown. Drain on absorbent paper, then serve as a snack or an accompaniment with Tandoori Jhinga (Tandoori king prawns (shrimp), see page 82, or Tandoori Chaamp (Tandoori lamb chops), see page 88, and a chutney or raita.

My Secrets

For a lighter, crispier batter, use half of the amount of water and make up the rest of the measurement with soda water or beer.

Ground rice adds a crispy texture to the fried batter. But if you do not have any, use fine semolina or cornmeal (polenta).

Aloo ke Tikkia

Spiced potato cakes

You must eat these fabulously flavoured potato cakes within 10–15 minutes of frying them. In my household they never last beyond that anyway! They are coated with vermicelli and deep-fried to give a rather inviting, rustic appearance.

In a large saucepan, boil the potatoes in plenty of water until tender. Drain and leave to cool slightly before peeling and roughly chopping them. Set aside.

Put one of the eggs and the bread in a food processor and whizz until the mixutre becomes fine. In a small bowl, beat the other 2 eggs together and set aside.

In a large mixing bowl, mash half the potatoes coarsely and set aside. Add the other batch of potatoes to the bread mixture in the food processor. Add the coriander (cilantro), mint, ginger, chillies and salt and process until all the ingredients are well blended. Add the onion and use the pulse action to chop it finely.

Transfer the mixture to the bowl of mashed potato, add the cheese and mix well. Divide it into 16 equally sized balls, then flatten them into round cakes.

Put the vermicelli in a plastic bag and crush coarsely with a rolling pin. In a wok or other pan suitable for deep-frying, heat the oil over a high heat.

Dip each potato cake in the beaten egg and roll in the crushed vermicelli. Working in batches if necessary, fry until browned on both sides and drain on absorbent paper. Serve with tomato ketchup or Tamatar ki Mithi Chutney ((Sweet tomato chutney), see page 142.

Makes 16

700 g/1½ lb potatoes

3 medium eggs

2 large slices white bread, crusts removed

2 tbsp coriander (cilantro) leaves and stalks, roughly chopped

2–3 tbsp fresh mint leaves

2.5 cm/1 in cube root ginger, roughly chopped

1–3 green chillies, chopped

1 tsp salt, or to taste

1 small red onion, roughly chopped

125 g/4 oz/½ cup mild cheddar cheese, grated

225 g/8 oz/1 cup rice vermicelli noodles

oil, for deep-frying

My Secret
Choosing the right kind of potato is important to achieve 100 per cent success. For this recipe, choose a floury variety such as King Edward, Desirée or Maris Piper.

Amritsari Machchi

Amritsar-style fish

Serves 4

700 g/1½ lb haddock fillets, cut into 7.5 cm/3 in pieces

juice of ½ lemon

1½ tsp salt, or to taste

125 g/4 oz/½ cup besan (gram flour), sieved

40 g/1½oz/3 tbsp cornflour (cornstarch)

½–1 tsp chilli powder

½ tsp aniseed

½ tsp ground turmeric

2.5 cm/1 in cube root ginger, finely grated

1 large egg, beaten

oil, for deep-frying

A popular dish from the excellent repertoire of the state of Punjab. I use haddock fillets for this recipe, but you can use any white fish. Try an Indian-style fish and chips and serve it with Tandoori Aloo (Tandoori potatoes), see page 81, cut into chip-shop style wedges. Koshimbir (Raw vegetable salad), see page 143, makes an excellent accompaniment. You could serve it as a side dish too.

Put the fish on a large plate and sprinkle with the lemon juice and half the salt. Set aside for 15 minutes.

In a mixing bowl, mix the besan with the remaining salt, cornflour (cornstarch), chilli powder, aniseed and turmeric. Add the ginger then gradually mix in 150 ml/5 fl oz/⅔ cup of water, stirring to give a thick paste. Stir in the beaten egg and mix until all the ingredients are well blended.

In a wok or other pan suitable for deep-frying, heat the oil over a high heat. When it reaches smoking point, reduce the heat slightly. Dip each piece of fish in the spiced batter and fry in the hot oil, taking care not to overcrowd the pan. Fry each batch for 3–4 minutes or until crisp and golden brown, then drain on absorbent paper.

My Secret

Whenever I buy fish in a supermarket, I am reminded of the beautiful fish found in the large lakes and rivers of North East India. These were brought straight to my grandmother's kitchen door, with glistening skin and bright eyes, and were cooked and consumed on the same day. To store any of the fish, my grandmother always sprinkled a little salt and turmeric over them to help preserve freshness then lightly fried them before storing in the fridge.

Kekda Tikki
Crab cakes

In the coastal region of India, especially in Kerala and Goa, seafood is found in abundance. As the claws are the meatiest part of the crab, deliciously spiced, coconut-based dishes are made using these. For this recipe, they believe only freshly cooked crab meat will do but I often use canned crab meat in brine for a quick and delicious alternative to fresh shellfish. Crab cakes make a delicious start to a meal when served with a salad.

In a frying pan, heat 1 tablespoon of the oil over a medium heat and fry the onion, ginger and garlic for 3–4 minutes or until the onions are soft. Remove from the heat.

Put the crab meat in a large mixing bowl and add the fried onion mixture and all the remaining ingredients. Mix thoroughly, then divide the mixture into 10 equal portions and flatten each one to a round cake about 1 cm/½ in thick.

Heat the oil over a medium-high heat in a wok or other pan suitable for deep-frying. Fry the cakes, without overcrowding the pan, until they are golden brown. Drain on absorbent paper. Serve hot or at room temperature.

Makes 10

sunflower oil, for frying

1 small red onion, finely chopped

2.5 cm/1 in cube root ginger, finely grated

2 cloves garlic, crushed

350 g/12 oz crab meat, well drained

1 large egg, beaten

40 g/1½ oz/¾ cup soft fresh breadcrumbs

2 tbsp coriander (cilantro) leaves, finely chopped

1 green chilli, finely chopped

½ tsp ground aniseed

½ tsp salt, or to taste

My Secret
If using canned crab meat, drain it well and add salt only if you want to. You can also use frozen crab meat for this recipe but you will need to thaw it completely and drain thoroughly before use.

Murgh Pakore

Spicy chicken fritters

Serves 4–6

375 g/12 oz skinned
chicken breast or thigh
fillets, cut into 2.5 cm/1 in
cubes

1 tbsp lemon juice

2–3 large cloves garlic,
crushed

2.5 cm/1 in cube root
ginger, finely grated

½–¾ tsp chilli powder

½ tsp ground cumin

½ tsp garam masala

1 tsp salt, or to taste

90 g/3½ oz/⅔ cup besan
(gram flour)

2 tbsp coriander (cilantro)
leaves and stalks, finely
chopped

½–¾ tsp crushed dried
chillies

a small pinch of
bicarbonate of soda

oi, for deep-frying

The appearance of these small chicken fritters will certainly make you stretch across the table to grab them! They are so delicious that the minute you take a bite you will know you are not going to stop at just one! Murgh Pakore was one of the favourite snacks during the British Raj and was enjoyed with a glass of chilled Sauterne wine.

Put the chicken in a non-corrosive mixing bowl and add the lemon juice, garlic, ginger, chilli powder, cumin and garam masala. Add half the salt and mix thoroughly. Leave to marinate for at least 2 hours, or refrigerate overnight but bring it to room temperature before cooking.

When ready to cook, in another mixing bowl, combine the reserved salt with the besan (gram flour), fresh coriander (cilantro), dried chillies and bicarbonate of soda and add the mixture to the chicken. Stir in 4 tablespoons of cold water and mix until the chicken pieces are coated with a thick batter that should resemble a paste.

Heat the oil in a wok or other suitable pan for deep frying over a medium heat. When hot, put in a few pieces of the coated chicken in a single layer, being sure not to overcrowd the pan. Fry for 5–6 minutes until golden brown. Drain on absorbent paper. Repeat with the rest of the chicken and serve.

My Secret
Batter using besan is quite sticky. Leave plenty of room to manoeuvre in the pan, otherwise the fritters will stick together.

Cocktail Koftas
Mini meatballs

Good things come in small packages, as the saying goes! These deliciously spiced, tender and tiny meatballs make a very welcoming snack. I have used chicken here, but you can use lamb or beef instead. Bread soaked in milk makes the meatballs deliciously tender.

Soak the bread in the milk for 2–3 minutes. Squeeze out all the milk and place the bread in a food processor, along with the remaining ingredients except the besan (gram flour) and oil. Blend the ingredients until smooth, then transfer to a bowl, cover and chill for at least 1 hour.

Heat enough oil in a karahi or wok for deep-frying. Make small, marble-sized balls from the chilled chicken mixture and roll them lightly in the besan. Fry the koftas in a single layer over a medium heat until browned. Drain on absorbent paper and serve with Aam ki Chutney (Mango dip), see page 145.

Serves 8–10

2 large slices 1–2 day old white bread, about 100 g/ 3½ oz, crusts removed

200 ml/7 fl oz/¾ cup milk

500g/1 lb skinned and boned chicken thighs, or minced (ground) chicken

2 tbsp double (heavy) cream

2 tbsp coriander (cilantro) leaves, chopped

3 large garlic cloves, crushed

1–2 green chillies, deseeded and chopped

2.5 cm/1 in cube root ginger, finely grated

1 tsp ground cumin

1 tsp garam masala

1 tsp salt, or to taste

½ tsp chilli powder

2 tbsp besan (gram flour)

sunflower oil, for frying

My Secrets
Chilling the meat mixture makes it easier to form the koftas. You can leave it for longer than an hour in the fridge – even overnight if you wish.

Koftas were introduced to India by the Middle Eastern invaders who used bulgar wheat to bind the meat. You can use this healthy ingredient if you do not have any besan. I often roll the meatballs lightly in cornflour (cornstarch) when I run out of besan.

Rice and Bread

Perfecting the essential staples

Rice and bread are the two starchy staples eaten all over India. Rice tends to be more popular in areas of abundant rainfall in the South, West and East, whilst bread is common in the drier, colder parts of Northern India.

Indian cuisine uses rice in a way no other cuisine does. Pulaos (pilau) ranging from very plain to utterly exotic, fabulous biryanis and simple flavoured rice dishes are all cooked to perfection transforming the grains in a way that delights a gourmet's palate.

Besides culinary uses, rice has religious and social significance in India. It is considered holy and a prasad (sacred offering) is cooked with rice, milk and sugar and offered to God during religious ceremonies. Rice symbolises good fortune and fertility in Hindu mythology. When a Hindu bridegroom arrives at the bride's house for the wedding ceremony, he is welcomed by the throwing of small handfuls of rice, rather like confetti in the West. During the ceremony, the bridal couple are asked to throw small handfuls of rice into the sacred fire, which is kept burning by the priest throughout the ceremony. At the end of the ceremony, when the bride leaves her parents' home and arrives at her husband's, a bowl of rice is offered to her before she enters the house. She then scatters some of it on the ground to indicate that she brings good fortune to her husband.

Bread can be made from different types of flour, the most common being wheat flour. Wheat flour is most commonly used for our unleavened flat breads, ranging from simple, fat-free chapatties to the rich, layered parathas which are made rather like flaky pastry. Leavened breads such as naan, of which there are numerous varieties, were brought to India by the Middle Eastern invaders. Flat breads are either dry-roasted or cooked with a small amount of oil or ghee. Some unleavened bread such as puris are deep-fried in a karahi (a small cast-iron wok).

Sada Pulao
Plain pilau rice

Most of you will be familiar with this pilau because Indian restaurant menus describe it as pilau rice. It is referred to as sada pulao or plain pilau because no meat, poultry, fish or vegetables are added to it. Apart from a few whole spices and a touch of turmeric, the delightful natural fragrance of the prized basmati rice is the main flavour of here.

Wash the rice in several changes of cold water then soak it in a bowl of fresh cold water for 30 minutes. Drain thoroughly.

In a heavy non-stick saucepan, heat the ghee or butter over a low heat and add the cinnamon, bay leaves, cardamom, cloves, peppercorns and cashews (if using). Stir-fry the ingredients gently for 25–30 seconds then add the rice, turmeric and salt and stir-fry for another 2–3 minutes.

Pour in 475 ml/16 fl oz/2 cups of hot water. Bring it to the boil and let cook, uncovered, for 2–3 minutes. Reduce the heat to low, cover the pan tightly and cook for 7–8 minutes. Remove from the heat and let stand for 5–6 minutes. Fluff up the pilau with a fork and transfer it to a serving dish. Serve with Aam ka Gosht (Lamb with mango), see page 39, Shabdegh (Slow-cooked lamb with turnips), see page 60. For a vegetarian meal, serve with Masoor Mussallam (Spiced whole red lentils), see page 20.

Serves 4

225 g/8 oz/1 cup basmati rice

2 tbsp ghee or unsalted butter

5 cm/2 in stick cinnamon

2 bay leaves, crumpled

4 each green cardamom pods, bruised

4 cloves

½ tsp black peppercorns

25 g/1 oz/2 tbsp raw cashew pieces (optional)

½ tsp ground turmeric

½ tsp salt

My Secret
Store rice in a cool dry place, preferably in an airtight container. In India, most families use special jute bags to store rice. If the rice is sold in a fabric bag, store it in that, but the polythene bags used to package the smaller quantities generally sold by supermarkets are not ideal.

Jeera Chawal

Cumin flavoured rice

Serves 4

225 g/8 oz/1 cup basmati rice

2 tbsp sunflower or vegetable oil

1 tsp cumin seeds

½ tsp black peppercorns

½ tsp salt, or to taste

Basmati rice, briefly stir-fried with cumin seeds and whole peppercorns, makes a wonderful accompaniment to any Indian dish.

Wash the rice until the water runs clear, then soak it in a bowl of fresh cold water for 30 minutes. Drain and set aside.

In a heavy non-stick saucepan, heat the oil over a medium heat and add the cumin and peppercorns. Stir-fry for 25–30 seconds, then add the rice and salt and stir-fry for 2–3 minutes.

Pour in 475 ml/16 fl oz/2 cups of hot water. Bring the rice to the boil and let it cook, uncovered, for 2–3 minutes. Reduce the heat to very low, cover the pan with a tight-fitting lid and cook for 7–8 minutes. Remove from the heat and allow to stand, undisturbed, for 5–6 minutes. Fluff up the rice with a fork and transfer to a serving dish.

My Secret
Cumin has wonderful digestive properties. It is a pungent spice without being harsh and can be used to add flavour to dishes that are mild or quite plain.

Kesar Pulao
Saffron pilau

Evocative saffron, with its beautiful vibrant colour, delicate appearance and intoxicating perfume, reigns supreme in the kingdom of spices. The secret of achieving its true colour, flavour and aroma is to be extremely light-handed in its use. This recipe is a classic example of combining two exquisite ingredients (basmati rice and saffron) to create a rare and harmonious beauty.

Wash the rice in several changes of water. In a bowl of fresh cold water, soak it for 30 minutes, then drain thoroughly.

In a heavy, non-stick saucepan, heat the ghee or butter over a low heat and fry the royal cumin and cardamom pods for 25–30 seconds. Add the rice and salt and stir-fry for 2–3 minutes.

Pour in 475 ml/16 fl oz/2 cups of hot water. Bring the rice to the boil and add the pounded saffron. Let cook, uncovered, for 2–3 minutes. Reduce the heat to very low, cover the pan tightly and cook for about 7–8 minutes.

Remove from the heat and leave the pan undisturbed for about 5–6 minutes. Fluff up the rice with a fork and transfer it to a serving dish. Garnish with the pistachios and serve with Dum ki Nalli (Slow-cooked lamb shanks), see page 59, or Dum Machchi (Fish baked in an aromatic sauce), see page 58, or any Korma dishes accompanied by a raita or a vegetable dish.

Serves 4

225 g/8 oz/1 cup basmati rice

2 tbsp ghee or unsalted butter

1 tsp royal cumin (shahi jeera), or caraway seeds

6 green cardamom pods, bruised

½ tsp salt

a small pinch of saffron strands, pounded

toasted pistachio nuts, lightly crushed, to garnish

My Secrets
When allowing cardamom pods to sizzle in the fat, make sure they swell up before you add the rice. When they are plump, they release their full flavour into the fat.

To extract full flavour and colour from saffron, Indian chefs heat it gently before pounding. The heating is generally done in the warm sunshine, but you can put the strands in the oven at the lowest setting. It only takes a few minutes.

Pudina-dhaniya ka Chawal

Mint and coriander (cilantro) rice

Serves 4

225 g/8 oz/1 cup basmati rice

2 tbsp sunflower or soya oil

5 cm/2 in stick cinnamon, halved

2 bay leaves

4 green cardamom pods, bruised

4 cloves

4 cloves garlic, cut into slivers

1–2 green chillies, deseeded and sliced

½ tsp ground turmeric

3 tbsp coriander (cilantro) leaves, finely chopped

2 tbsp fresh mint, finely chopped or 1 tsp dried mint

1 tsp salt, or to taste

2 tbsp pine nuts

Here I have combined two exquisite ingredients from the Himalayan region, basmati rice and pine nuts. As a child growing up in the foothills of the Himalayas, I remember going into the pine forests to collect the ripe cones. In the refreshing cold air with its heady bouquet of pine trees, it was a joy to open the cones which revealed long, slender nuts. In this recipe, they are perfectly matched with the equally long and slender basmati rice and its enchanting aroma.

Wash the rice gently in plenty of cold water until the water runs clear. Place in a bowl, cover with fresh water and soak for 30 minutes. Drain thoroughly.

In a heavy saucepan, heat the oil over low heat and add the cinnamon, bay leaves, cardamom and cloves. Fry gently for 20–25 seconds, then add the garlic and chillies. Continue frying until the garlic turns light brown.

Add the rice and turmeric to the saucepan, increase the heat to medium and stir-fry for 2–3 minutes. Add 475 ml/16 fl oz/2 cups of lukewarm water, plus the coriander (cilantro), mint and salt. Stir once and bring to the boil. Let boil for 2–3 minutes, then reduce the heat to very low, cover the pan tightly and cook for 7–8 minutes. Switch off the heat and let the rice stand, undisturbed, for 5–6 minutes.

Meanwhile, preheat a small heavy pan over a medium heat and dry-roast the pine nuts until they begin to glisten with their natural oils and brown slightly. Transfer to a plate and leave to cool.

Fluff up the rice with a fork and put into a serving dish. Scatter the roasted pine nuts on top and serve with Firdausi Qorma (Heavenly korma), see page 73.

My Secret

If you are worried about being able to maintain the heat at the minimum level, use a heat diffuser. Alternatively, transfer the fried rice to a microwavable dish and add boiling rather than lukewarm water. Cover the dish with plastic wrap that has been punctured, or use a plate. Cook for 4 minutes on high then 6 minutes on low or simmer (800 watt output). Let it stand for 5–6 minutes before stirring in the pine nuts.

Mewa Pulao
Dry fruit pilau

Kashmir, surrounded by the snow-capped peaks of the Himalayas, produces a wealth of beautiful fruits during the summer months and Kashmiri cuisine makes lavish use of fruits and nuts. I have exciting childhood memories of Kashmiri traders coming down to the foothills with succulent and lustrous fruits. Here is a deliciously fruity pilau rice from that region.

Wash the rice in several changes of water until the water runs clear. Soak in a bowl of fresh cold water for 30 minutes, then drain. Meanwhile, soak the pounded saffron in the hot milk and set aside.

In a heavy saucepan, heat the oil over low heat and add the chillies, cinnamon, royal cumin, cardamom and cloves. Stir-fry them gently for 25–30 seconds, then add the walnuts and almonds. Continue frying for a further 30–40 seconds.

Add the drained rice, apricots, prunes, salt and 475 ml/16 fl oz/ 2 cups of lukewarm water. Stir once, bring to the boil and cover the pan tightly. Reduce the heat to the lowest setting, cover and cook for 10 minutes without lifting the lid.

Sprinkle the saffron milk randomly over the cooked rice and switch off the heat. Cover the pan and leave it undisturbed for 8–10 minutes. Stir the rice gently and transfer to a serving dish. Serve with Assado de Leitoa (Goan spicy roast pork), see page 89.

Serves 4

225 g/8 oz/1 cup basmati rice

a large pinch of saffron strands, pounded

2 tbsp hot milk

4 tbsp sunflower or soya oil

1–2 green chillies, deseeded and finely chopped

5 cm/2 in stick cinnamon, halved

1 tsp royal cumin (shahi jeera)

4 green cardamom pods, bruised

4 cloves

25 g/1 oz/2 tbsp walnut pieces

25 g/1 oz/2 tbsp slivered almonds

25 g/1 oz/2 tbsp ready-to-eat dried apricots, sliced

25 g/1 oz/2 tbsp ready-to-eat prunes, sliced

1 tsp salt, or to taste

My Secrets
If you find it difficult to achieve beautifully cooked rice with dry and separate grains, here is one of the secrets which will never let you down. Always wash the rice by rubbing the grains very gently until the water runs clear. Once washed, soak it for 20–30 minutes then drain thoroughly. This will remove most of the milling starch which can make the rice sticky when cooked. Because the grains have been moistened and softened, they will be able to absorb the water more easily during the cooking process. At the end of the resting period, stir the rice gently with a flat metal or plastic spoon as wooden ones will squash the fragile grains.

Mattar-paneer ka Pulao

Pilau rice with peas and Indian cheese

Serves 4

225 g/8 oz/1cup basmati rice

4 tbsp sunflower or soya oil

125 g/4 oz/½ cup paneer or halloumi cheese, cut into bite-size pieces

5 cm/2 in stick cinnamon, halved

2 bay leaves, crumpled

1 tsp royal cumin (shahi jeera)

6 green cardamom pods, bruised

6 cloves

1 medium onion, finely sliced

1 green chilli, deseeded and finely chopped

1 tsp salt, or to taste

½ tsp ground turmeric

150 g/5 oz/⅔ cup frozen petits pois

2 fresh red chillies, deseeded and cut into strips

2 tbsp coriander (cilantro) leaves, finely chopped

Paneer is available in all Indian stores and some of the larger supermarkets. It has a bland taste and the ability to absorb flavours easily and quickly. Cyprus halloumi cheese is a good alternative.

Wash the rice gently in several changes of water, then soak in a bowl of cold water for 30 minutes. Drain and set aside.

In a non-stick frying pan, heat 1 tablespoon of the oil over a medium heat and fry the cheese until browned all over, stirring frequently. Drain on absorbent paper.

In a heavy saucepan, heat the remaining oil over a low heat and add the cinnamon, bay leaves, royal cumin, cardamom and cloves. Stir-fry for 15–20 seconds. Add the onion and chilli, increase the heat to medium and fry, stirring frequently, for 8–9 minutes until the onion is soft and light brown.

Stir in the salt and turmeric, then add the drained rice, fried cheese and petit pois. Fry for 2–3 minutes. Pour in 475 ml/16 fl oz/2 cups of hot water. Bring to the boil and cook for 1 minute, then reduce the heat to very low and cover the pan tightly. Cook for 12 minutes without lifting the lid.

Switch off the heat and leave the pilau undisturbed for 8-10 minutes. Using a metal spoon, transfer the rice to a serving dish and garnish with the chillies and coriander (cilantro).

My Secrets

Freshly cooked rice, especially basmati, is very fragile, so for perfect results, let it rest undisturbed for a few minutes after cooking.

Stand away from the pan while frying the cheese as it has a tendency to splatter in hot fat.

Kheema Pulao
Pilau rice with spiced lamb

Pulaos and biryanis are among the fine range of dishes contributed by the Moguls to Indian cuisine. Mogul Emperor Jahangir once described rice as 'the most wonderful gift of nature' and 'worth its weight in gold'. Here the alluring aroma of the exquisite and slender grains of basmati provides a luxurious background to the spiced minced (ground) meat.

Wash the rice until the water runs clear then soak in a bowl of cold water for 30 minutes. Drain and set aside.

Meanwhile, put the minced (ground) meat and milk in a saucepan over a medium heat and cook, uncovered, for 10 minutes or until the meat is dry and crumbly. Drain off the excess fat.

Grind the poppy, sunflower and coriander seeds in a coffee grinder or spice mill until fine.

In a heavy, non-stick saucepan, heat the oil over a low heat and add the cinnamon, bay leaves. cardamom, cloves and peppercorns. Let them sizzle for 25–30 seconds then add the onion. Increase the heat to medium and fry for 10–12 minutes, stirring frequently, until the onion is browned.

Add the ginger, garlic and green chillies. Fry for 1 minute then add the ground seeds and fry for a further minute. Add the meat and turmeric and continue to cook, stirring constantly, for 2–3 minutes.

Add the rice, tomato and salt and stir-fry for 1 minute. Pour in 600 ml/1 pint/2½ cups of hot water. Bring to the boil and cook for 2–3 minutes. Reduce the heat to very low. Cover the pan with a piece of foil then place the lid on and cook for 12–15 minutes. Remove the pan from the heat and let it stand, undisturbed, for 5–6 minutes.

Carefully transfer the rice to a serving dish and serve garnished with the toasted almonds.

My Secrets

The mince will form lumps while it is cooking in the milk. Break up some of them, but leave some intact to help give texture to the pilau.

For a striking appearance in true Mogul style, scatter 2–3 tablespoons of pomegranate seeds on the pilau before serving.

Serves 4

225 g/8 oz/1 cup basmati rice

500 g/1 lb minced (ground) lamb, beef or chicken

150 ml/5 fl oz/⅔ cup whole milk

1 tbsp white poppy seeds

1 tbsp sunflower seeds

2 tsps coriander seeds

3–4 tbsp sunflower or vegetable oil

5 cm/2 in stick cinnamon

2 bay leaves, crumpled

4 green cardamom pods, bruised

4 cloves

½ tsp black peppercorns

1 large onion, finely sliced

2.5 cm/1 in cube root ginger, finely grated

5–6 large cloves garlic, crushed

1–3 green chillies, finely chopped

½ tsp ground turmeric

1 tomato, skinned, deseeded and chopped

1½ tsp salt, or to taste

toasted flaked almonds, to garnish

Masala Puri
Deep-fried puffed bread

Makes 16

275 g/10 oz/2½ cups plain (all-purpose) flour, plus extra for dusting

½ tsp crushed dried red chillies

½ tsp royal cumin (shahi jeera), or caraway seeds

½ tsp dried mint

½ tsp onion seeds (kalonji)

½ tsp salt

½ tsp sugar

1 tbsp ghee, butter or margarine

sunflower oil, for deep-frying

Puris can be made with either plain (all-purpose) or wholemeal (wholewheat) flour. Although Indian wholemeal flour (atta) is more nourishing than regular plain or wholemeal flour, I have chosen plain flour for this recipe. Its white colour is visually more appealing when adorned with the tiny black onion seeds, royal cumin and flakes of red chilli. They also taste absolutely yummy.

Sieve the flour into a large bowl and add all the dry ingredients. Mix well then rub in the fat with your fingertips. Gradually add about 175 ml/6 fl oz/¾ cup of lukewarm water, or enough to make a stiff dough. Transfer to a flat surface and knead for 4–5 minutes. Alternatively, make the dough in a food processor, mixing the dry ingredients together first. Cover the dough with a damp cloth and allow to rest for 20–30 minutes.

Divide the dough into two equal parts and then make 8 equal sized balls from each. Flatten the balls between your palms, rotating and pressing them to form flat discs. Cover with a damp cloth.

Heat the oil in a wok or other pan suitable for deep frying over a medium-high heat. Meanwhile, start rolling out the puris. Dust each cake very lightly with flour and roll out to a disc of about 7.5 cm/3 in diameter, taking care not to tear or pierce the dough. Place in a single layer on a piece of greaseproof paper and cover with another piece.

When the oil has a faint shimmer of rising smoke on the surface, carefully drop in one puri and, as soon as it floats, gently tap it around the edges to encourage puffing. When it has puffed up, turn it over and fry the other side until browned. Drain on absorbent paper. Keep the fried puris on a tray in a single layer. Eat them fresh, or re-heat them briefly (4–5 minutes) in a hot oven. Serve with any tandoori dishes, kebabs and bhuna dishes with little or no sauce.

My Secrets
The exact amount of water you will need to form a stiff dough will depend on the absorbency of the flour and the storage temperature. It is important not to tear or pierce the dough while rolling the puris as they will not puff up if damaged.

To make sure that the oil is at the right temperature, break off a tiny piece of the dough and drop into the hot oil. If the dough floats quickly without browning, then the oil is at the right temperature.

Crushed chillies can be made by grinding dried red chillies in a spice mill. You could use bought red chilli paste instead.

Sheermal
Milk bread

This rich Muslim speciality which originated in Kashmir is definitely a dinner party recipe. The bread looks superb with saffron threads and royal cumin adorning the surface.

Put the flour, sugar, baking powder and salt in a large mixing bowl and mix well. Add half the melted margarine and work it into the flour with your fingertips. Then work in the cream. Reserve 4 tablespoons of the milk and gradually add the remainder to the flour mixture. Knead until a soft dough is formed.

Add the remaining melted margarine and knead until the dough is smooth and velvety. If you are mixing by hand, transfer the dough to a pastry board to knead. Cover the dough with a slightly damp cloth and allow to rest for 30 minutes.

Meanwhile, preheat the oven to 220°C/425°F/Gas 7. Line a baking sheet with a piece of greased greaseproof paper or non-stick baking parchment. In a small saucepan, heat the reserved milk to boiling point and soak the pounded saffron in it for 10–15 minutes.

Divide the dough into 8 equal pieces, roll them into balls and flatten each one to a round cake. Dust each cake lightly in flour and roll out to about 20 cm/8 in diameter. Carefully lift and place on the prepared baking sheet – you should be able to bake 2–3 sheermal at a time, depending on the size of the baking sheet.

Brush the surface generously with the saffron-flavoured milk and sprinkle with a little royal cumin or caraway seeds. Bake on a high shelf for 7–8 minutes or until browned.

Line a piece of foil with kitchen paper and place the cooked sheermal at one end. Fold the lined foil over to keep the bread warm while baking the remainder. Once you have finished baking them all, seal the edges of the foil to keep them warm.

Makes 8

500 g/1 lb/3 cups plain (all-purpose) white flour, plus extra for dusting

1 tbsp sugar

1 tsp baking powder

1 tsp salt

125 g/4 oz/½ cup sunflower margarine, melted

150 ml/5 fl oz/¼ cup half-fat single (light) cream

225 ml/8 fl oz/1 cup warm semi-skimmed (low-fat) milk

1 tsp saffron threads, pounded

1 tbsp royal cumin (shahi jeera) or caraway seeds

My Secrets
When mixing the dough, the milk should not be added all at once. Blending is done more evenly if it is added gradually.

A good way to determine whether the dough has been kneaded enough, is when it stops sticking to the board and your fingers. If you use a food processor, make sure the dough stops sticking to the dough hook and the bowl. Once the dough appears non-sticky, you can test it further by pressing it lightly: if it springs back it is kneaded fully.

Roghani Roti

Creamy rich bread

Makes 12

250 g/9 oz/1¾ cups plain (all-purpose) flour, plus extra for dusting

250 g/9 oz/1¾ cups atta, chapatti or wholemeal (wholewheat) flour

½ tsp salt

70 g/2½ oz/¼ cup butter

150 ml/5 fl oz/⅔ cup double (heavy) cream

oil or melted butter, for brushing

Roti is a generic name for all Indian flat breads. This particular unleavened bread is rather rich, with a soft, velvety texture that literally melts in your mouth.

In a large mixing bowl, combine both types of four and the salt. Rub in the butter and, when it is fully incorporated, add the cream and mix well. Gradually add 150–175 ml/5-6 fl oz/⅔–¾ cup of lukewarm water and mix to form a dough. Transfer to a board and knead for 3–4 minutes. Alternatively, make the dough in a food processor. Cover with a damp cloth and set aside for 20–30 minutes.

Divide the dough into two equal parts and make 6 balls from each. Flatten them into cakes by rotating and pressing the dough between your palms. Cover the cakes with a slightly damp cloth.

Have ready a piece of greaseproof paper large enough to hold 3–4 rotis in a single layer. Dust each cake lightly with flour and roll out to a disc of about 18 cm/7 in diameter.

Preheat a heavy griddle or frying pan over a medium heat and place a roti on it. Cook for 30–40 seconds then turn it over and cook for about 1 minute. At the same time, brush the first cooked side with a little oil or butter. Turn the bread over and brush the second side with oil or butter and cook until browned. Repeat the process with the remaining breads.

My Secrets

You can roll and cook the breads simultaneously to save time – there is ample time to do this as you can see from the cooking instructions above. But if you find it easier to roll them all out first, layer them in batches of 3 or 4 between large sheets of greaseproof paper.

As a young girl I learned from my mother never to wash my tawa (griddle). To keep hers in peak condition, my mother always wiped it clean after use, then rubbed a little oil on the surface before putting it away.

Tandoori King Prawns (page 82)

Fish Korma (page 68) and Mint and Coriander Rice (page 122)

Spiced Minced Lamb Patties (page 100) and Sag Aloo (page 52)

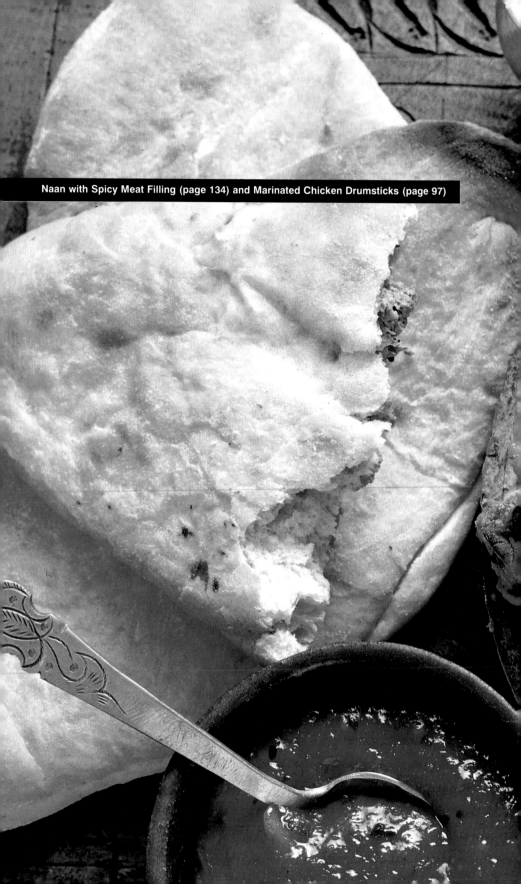

Naan with Spicy Meat Filling (page 134) and Marinated Chicken Drumsticks (page 97)

Chocolate Ice Cream with Mandarin Sauce (page 150)

Chukander ki Roti

Beetroot bread

Indian cuisine boasts a sensational range of bread of nearly a hundred varieties, yet in the Indian restaurants of the West we are offered only a few stereotypical ones. Indian housewives make fresh bread for each meal. Here is an unusual recipe that is as delicious as it is healthy, but it is also time-efficient as no proving is required. Generally, unleavened bread, especially chapatti, is eaten every day and is at its best when freshly made.

Sieve both types of flour into a large mixing bowl and add the cumin, salt and pepper. Mix well, then add the oil and grated beetroot (beet). Gradually add 175 ml/6 fl oz/¾ cup of lukewarm water and mix until you have a soft dough. Transfer to a flat surface and knead by hand for 3–4 minutes until the dough is smooth and pliable. Alternatively, make the dough in a food processor. Cover with a damp cloth and allow to rest for 20–30 minutes.

Divide the dough into two equal parts and make six balls out of each. Flatten them by rotating and pressing them between your palms, keeping the flattened cakes covered. Dust each cake lightly in flour and roll out to a circle of 18 cm/7 in diameter.

Preheat a heavy griddle or frying pan over a medium heat and place a round of bread on it. Cook for 30 seconds and turn it over. Allow to cook for about 1 minute while you brush the top surface with some oil. Turn the bread over again, brush the other side with oil and cook until browned on both sides.

Makes 12

225 g/8 oz/1 cup atta, chapatti or wholemeal (wholewheat) flour

225 g/8 oz/1 cup plain (all-purpose) flour, plus extra for dusting

1 tsp cumin seeds, crushed

1 tsp salt

½ tsp freshly milled black pepper

2 tbsp sunflower or soya oil

2 small raw beetroots (beets), about 175 g/ 6 oz/¾ cup, finely grated

sunflower oil, for brushing

My Secrets

Rolling out the rotis and cooking can be done simultaneously. You can, of course, roll out all the rotis first – see the instructions given for Roghani Roti (Creamy rich bread), see page 128.

If you do not want to serve the breads immediately, you can keep them hot for about 30 minutes. Line a piece of foil with absorbent paper and wrap the breads well. Seal the parcel completely by folding the edges of the foil.

Palak Puri

Deep-fried puffed bread with spinach

Makes 18

2 tbsp sunflower or vegetable oil

½ tsp aniseed

½ tsp onion seeds (kalonji)

175g/6 oz/¾ cup fresh or thawed frozen spinach leaves, finely chopped

1 tsp ground cumin

½ tsp chilli power

½ tsp salt

375g/12 oz/2½ cups atta, chapatti or wholemeal (wholewheat) flour

oil, for deep-frying

Hot puffy bread with a cool green colour and a touch of spices; these are definitely to die for! Even if you do not like spinach, I am sure that once you have tasted these puris, you will want to repeat the sensational experience!

In a medium saucepan, heat the sunflower or vegetable oil over a moderate heat. When hot but not smoking, add the aniseed and onion seeds. Let them sizzle for 15–20 seconds, then add the spinach, cumin, chilli powder and salt. Toss them around in the pan until the leaves wilt, then remove from the heat.

Put the flour in a large mixing bowl and add the spinach mixture and 1 tablespoon of water. Mix until a stiff dough is formed. Transfer to a board and knead until pliable. Alternatively, make the dough using a food processor. Cover the dough with a damp cloth and leave to rest for 20–30 minutes.

Divide the dough into 2 parts and make 9 lime-sized balls out of each. In a wok or other pan suitable for deep-frying, heat some oil over a medium-high heat. Line a large tray with absorbent kitchen paper. While the oil is heating, roll out as many puris as you can, to discs of about 7.5 cm/3 in diameter. Spread them on a sheet of greaseproof paper in a single layer.

As soon as the oil reaches smoking point, carefully drop a puri in it. As soon as the puri floats on the surface, gently tap it round the edges to encourage it to puff up. When it has puffed up, turn it over and fry until the second side is brown. Drain on the paper-lined tray.

Fry all the puris the same way and keep them in the tray in a single layer. Serve with kababs or tandoori dishes.

My Secrets

Take care not to damage the puris when rolling them out because if torn or damaged they will not puff up. If your puris do not puff up, to make it less obvious, you can use them to wrap kababs or tandoori dishes. Spread a chutney on the meat before wrapping.

Before you use a wok or a griddle, you need to season it. To do this, wash the pan in hot soapy water. Place it over a high heat and add a little oil. When the oil starts smoking, switch off the heat source and swirl the hot oil on the surface of the pan. Let cool, then wipe with kitchen paper. Do this at regular intervals to look after your pan.

Lasoon ki Roti

Garlic bread

This garlic flavoured flat bread with plenty of freshly ground black pepper will bring your taste buds alive in a hurry! They are perfect with just about any Indian dish.

In a small saucepan, heat the butter over a low heat and fry the garlic gently until light brown. Remove from the heat.

In a large mixing bowl, mix the flour with coriander (cilantro), pepper and salt, then add the garlic butter. Mix thoroughly and gradually add 7–8 fl oz/200–225 ml/¾–1 cup of lukewarm water to form a dough. Transfer to a board and knead until soft and pliable. Alternatively, make the dough in a food processor. Cover with a damp cloth and let it rest for 20–30 minutes.

Make 12 equal-sized balls out of the dough and flatten them into round cakes, keeping them covered with a slightly damp cloth. Dust each cake lightly in flour and roll out to a disc of about 18 cm/ 7 in diameter.

Preheat a griddle or large heavy frying pan over a medium heat and place a roti on it. Cook for about 30 seconds then turn it over with a thin spatula or fish slice. Let the second side cook for about 1 minute then brush a little oil over the side you cooked first. Turn the bread over and brush the second side with oil too. Cook until both sides have brown patches and serve hot.

Makes 10

4 tbsp unsalted butter

8 large cloves garlic, crushed

500 g/1 lb 2oz/3¼ cups atta, chapatti or wholemeal (wholewheat) flour, plus extra for dusting

2–3 tbsp coriander (cilantro) leaves, finely chopped

1–1½ tsps freshly ground black pepper

1 tsp salt

oil, for shallow frying

My Secrets
As it is difficult to be precise about the quantity of water required, add it gradually to the flour. The absorbency level varies with different types of flour.

To keep the cooked breads hot, wrap them in a large piece of foil lined with absorbent paper. Fold in the edges to seal completely. If you need to reheat them, place the foil package in the centre of a moderate oven for 10–12 minutes then serve immediately.

Methi Na Thepla

Fenugreek flat bread

Makes 12

500g/1 lb 2 oz/3¼ cups atta, chapatti or wholemeal (wholewheat) flour, plus extra for dusting

1 tbsp dried fenugreek leaves, stalks removed

1 tsp ground coriander

1 tsp ground cumin

1 tsp salt

½ tsp chilli powder

½ tsp ground turmeric

2 tbsp sunflower or vegetable oil, plus extra for frying and brushing

Thepla, a spicy flat bread from Gujarat in Western India, is similar to a chapatti, the everyday bread of Indian homes. Good enough to eat on their own, theplas are made quite thin and shallow-fried to give a crisp texture. Fresh fenugreek leaves are normally used for this bread, but my recipe uses dried fenugreek (kasuri methi) as it keeps well and I do not have to make a special trip to an Indian store when I want to eat this gorgeous bread.

In a large mixing bowl, mix the flour with the other dry ingredients. Rub in 2 tablespoons of the oil. Gradually add 300 ml/½ pint/1¼ cups of lukewarm water and mix until a dough is formed. Transfer to a board, add the remaining oil and knead for 4–5 minutes. Alternatively, make the dough in a food processor. Cover with a slightly damp cloth and leave to rest for 20–30 minutes.

Divide the dough into 12 equal-sized balls and flatten each one to a thick cake. Dust lightly with flour and roll out thinly to discs of about 20 cm/8 in diameter.

Preheat a griddle or heavy frying pan over a high heat. Place a rolled thepla on it and dry-roast for 30–35 seconds. Turn it over and spread about 1 tablespoon of oil all the way around the thepla, gently rubbing a little oil on the surface as well. Fry for 30–35 seconds then lift slightly to check if brown patches have appeared on the underside. If so, turn it over and repeat with the oil. Cook until brown patches have appeared on the other side and remove the bread from the pan.

My Secrets

Indian homes use a tawa for cooking these flat breads but you can use a griddle instead. One without rasied edges is most convenient. A heavy frying pan or skillet will also do.

Sometimes I use 3 or 4 of the flat cakes to make a quick snack to serve with drinks. Roll them out as above, then cut them into small square or triangular pieces. Deep-fry until crisp and golden brown and drain on absorbent paper. They will keep well for about 10 days in an airtight container.

Andey ki Roti
Bread with spiced eggs

Wholewheat flour, lightly spiced potatoes and eggs make this a wholesome bread that is a meal in itself.

Mix the flour and 1 teaspoon of the salt in a large bowl. Add the oil, mix well then gradually add 300 ml/½ pint/1¼ cups of lukewarm water and mix to a soft dough. Transfer to a flat surface and knead for 4–5 minutes until pliable.

Meanwhile, boil the potatoes in a large saucepan of water. Cool then peel and mash them. Add 1 teaspoon of salt plus the chillies, half the coriander (cilantro), mint, onion and ginger. Mix thoroughly and divide the mixture into 10 equal-sized portions.

In a small bowl, beat the eggs and then stir in the remaining coriander (cilantro) and ½ teaspoon of salt. Preheat a griddle or heavy frying pan over a low heat.

Cut the dough into 10 equal portions and roll out each piece on a well-floured board to a circle with a diameter of 20 cm/8 in. Place a portion of the potato mixture in the centre and spread it out with the back of a spoon leaving a 2.5 cm/1 in border all the way round the bread. Fold the edges over the filling so that you end up with a square and approximately 7.5 cm/3 in of the filling is visible.

Lift the filled bread gently and place it on the hot griddle. Pour 2 tablespoons of the beaten egg mixture over the filling and the border to seal it. Spread 1 tablespoon of oil around the edges of the bread. Let it cook for 3–4 minutes then turn it over with a wide spatula or egg flip and cook for another minute so that the egg sets. Pour another tablespoon of oil around the edges as before and press the sides down with the spatula so that they cook evenly.

Cook for another 4–5 minutes until browned, then serve on its own for a light lunch or add a vegetable curry to make a complete meal.

My Secret
Once you have filled the rotis, you can stack them on a large plate lined with greaseproof paper placing a sheet of greaseproof paper between each layer. Place some absorbent paper on the top sheet of greaseproof paper and cover the whole lot with plastic wrap. Refrigerate overnight and complete the recipe next day when you are ready to serve the meal. You can also freeze these breads once they are filled.

Makes 10

500g/1 lb 2 oz/3¼ cups atta, chapatti or wholemeal (wholewheat) flour, plus extra for dusting

2½ tsps salt

3 tbsp sunflower or soya oil, plus extra for frying

500 g/1 lb potatoes

1–3 green chillies, deseeded and finely chopped

4 tbsp coriander (cilantro) leaves, finely chopped

2 tbsp fresh mint, finely chopped or ½ tsp dried mint

2–3 tbsp red onion, very finely chopped

1 cm/½ in cube root ginger, finely grated

5 large eggs, beaten

Kheema Naan

Naan with spicy meat filling

Makes 6

For the bread:

500 g/1 lb/2 cups self-raising flour, plus extra for dusting

7 g/¼oz/1 sachet easy-blend dried yeast

2 tsp sugar

1 tsp salt

6 tbsp ghee or unsalted butter

225 ml/8 fl oz/1 cup soda water (seltzer)

oil, for brushing

For the filling:

500 g/1 lb lean minced (ground) lamb or beef

1 medium egg

A meal in itself, soft, fluffy kheema naan is a delicious treat any time! Although the recipe may seem long, it is fairly easy to make. The dough takes little time, especially if you use a food processor, and the filling needs no precooking.

Mix all the dry ingredients for the dough in a large mixing bowl and rub in the fat. Gradually add the soda water (seltzer) and mix to a soft, sticky dough. Transfer to a flat surface and knead until the dough stops sticking to your fingers and the work surface. Alternatively, make the dough in a food processor, mixing the dry ingredients first; the dough is ready when it stops sticking to the sides of the bowl.

Put the dough in a large plastic food bag and tie up the opening. Place it in a warmed bowl and leave in a warm place for a couple of hours.

Meanwhile, put all the ingredients for the filling in a food processor and blend until the mixture is smooth. Transfer to a bowl, cover and chill for about 1 hour.

Knock back the dough and divide it into 6 equal portions. Cover and set aside to prove for 15–20 minutes.

Preheat the oven to 220°C/425°C/Gas 7. Line a large baking tray (cookie sheet) with greased greaseproof paper or non-stick baking parchment.

My Secret
The three stages (mixing, kneading and resting) of making a traditional Indian bread are extremely important. While mixing, water is added accurately to ensure a firm dough that is nevertheless soft and pliable. Kneading is traditionally done by hand using the knuckles and could take as long as 10 minutes. Resting is important because during kneading the gluten in the flour is activated and resting the dough will enable it to relax, thereby making it less resistant to rolling and stretching.

Divide the filling into 6 equal parts. Take a piece of dough and flatten it by stretching and patting until it is large enough to enclose a portion of the filling. Place the filling in the centre and seal the edges tightly. Flatten it gently into a flat cake and dust it with flour. Roll it out carefully to a 12.5 cm/5 in disc. Place one hand on the top of the disc and gently pull the lower end with the other to make a tear-drop shape, if desired (round naans are perfectly acceptable). Repeat with the remaining dough and filling.

Place 2–3 naans on the baking tray and brush the surface with oil. Bake on a high shelf for 9–10 minutes, then repeat with the remaining naans. Serve with raita and/or chutney for a complete meal or as a part of a dinner party menu.

1 small red onion, roughly chopped

2–3 large cloves garlic, roughly chopped

1–2 green chillies, roughly chopped

2.5 cm/1 in cube root ginger, roughly chopped

3–4 tbsp coriander (cilantro) leaves and stalks, roughly chopped

2 tbsp fresh mint, or 1½ tsp dried mint

1 tbsp ground coriander

2 tsp garam masala

1 tsp salt, or to taste

Salads and Chutneys

Complementing your meal

No Indian meal is complete without these inviting little side dishes, but there is much more to Indian relishes than the perennially popular mango chutney and lime pickle. In this section you will find raitas (salads) and chutneys which perhaps you may not have come across before. I have endeavoured to give you some totally different recipes, most of which come from my family's kitchens in the North and North East, and along the West Coast of India where my husband's family comes from.

I fondly remember my mother carefully picking fresh spinach leaves, mint, coriander (cilantro) and other greens typical of this region from the garden and making mouth-watering relishes. These were sometimes sweetened with jaggery (unrefined palm sugar), salted with rock salt and soured with tamarind picked from the huge tamarind tree in our back garden. They had the additional advantages of home-grown garlic and fiery red and green chillies! When these were ground on the traditional grinding stone, the air was filled with a magical aroma. Somehow, today's modern gadgets don't appear to have the same effect!

Cooking in my part of the country is high on herbs. Fresh herbs are used in most recipes and raitas and chutneys are made from these every day. As is the traditional Indian way of serving, the main meal was surrounded by various dry and semi-dry dishes, which were accompanied by delicious relishes.

In Goa, Bombay and Pune, where most of my husband's family live, raw vegetables and fruits are used to make the chutneys. Coconut is used quite freely because of its abundance along the coastal area. The fruits and vegetables are cut into small pieces, lightly flavoured with spices and left to stand so that the juices released by them can be blended to make unique dressings. The fresh produce is also coated with a lightly seasoned plain yogurt dressing to make delicious raitas.

Gajjar-palak ka Raita
Carrot and spinach in spiced yogurt

This is one of my favourite raitas. Emerald green, tender spinach leaves and the soft orange colour of the carrots look quite spectacular against the snow white plain yogurt. A hot oil seasoning of nutty mustard seeds and warm, assertive cumin seeds, transforms this simple dish into a real delight for the eye as well as the palate.

Steam the carrots until al dente and allow to cool thoroughly.

Meanwhile, in a coffee grinder or spice mill, grind the coconut until fine. Transfer to a mixing bowl and add the green chilli. Pour in 125 ml/4 fl oz/½ cup of boiling water, cover and set aside for 10–12 minutes.

In a large mixing bowl, whisk the yogurt and soured cream together until smooth. Add the salt, cooled carrots and the coconut mixture and mix thoroughly. Lightly fold in the spinach leaves.

In a small steel ladle, heat the oil over a medium heat. When hot, add the mustard seeds followed by the cumin. As soon as they begin to crackle, pour the entire contents of the ladle over the raita, mix gently and serve.

Serves 4

225 g/8 oz/1 cup carrots, peeled and cut into bite-size pieces

25 g/1 oz/2 tbsp unsweetened desiccated coconut

1 green chilli, deseeded and finely chopped

125 g/4 oz/½ cup whole milk plain yogurt

4 tbsp soured cream

½ tsp salt

90 g/3 oz/⅓ cup finely shredded baby spinach leaves

2 tsp sunflower or soya oil

½ tsp black mustard seeds

½ tsp cumin seeds

My Secrets
To bring out the full flavour of the seeds, let the oil come to smoking point, switch off the heat source, then add them.

To create a more appetizing look reserve a little of the seasoned oil and seeds. When the raita is ready, drizzle it over and serve.

Pudina-piaz ki Chutney

Mint and onion chutney

Serves 4–6

2 tbsp sunflower or
vegetable oil

½ tsp onion seeds (kalonji)

1 large onion, roughly
chopped

15 g/½ oz/¾ cup fresh mint
leaves

1–2 fresh red chillies,
chopped

1 tbsp lime juice

½ tsp salt, or to taste

*A fabulously fragrant chutney in which the predominant flavours
come from the fresh chillies and mint leaves. The white and green
background is speckled with fresh red chillies and black onion seeds,
which make it look very inviting. It keeps well in an airtight jar in the
fridge for 3–4 weeks.*

In a small saucepan, heat the oil over a medium heat. Add the onion
seeds, then the onion and fry for 3–4 minutes. Reduce the heat
slightly and continue frying for 5 minutes or until the onion is soft but
not brown.

Remove the onion from the heat and let it cool. Purée in a blender
with the mint, chillies, lime juice and salt. Transfer to a dry airtight jar
and refrigerate.

My Secrets

If the onion begins to brown, reduce the heat to low. The onion juices
must evaporate completely to boost the life of the chutney.

To transform the appearance, taste and texture of this chutney,
scatter a few pomegranate seeds on top before serving. The fruit's
remaining seeds, besides being good enough to eat on their own,
can be used in fruit salads or as a garnish for pilau rice. In days gone
by, Indian women have used the juice of pomegranate seeds as an
effective beauty aid. It is believed to contain astringent as well as
clarifying qualities.

Simla Mirch ka Raita

Sweet peppers in spiced yogurt

During the school holidays, visiting the open air market with my mother, was one of the highlights of my day. Sweet bell peppers came from Simla, in the hilly Northern Terrain, and the tribal women brought them down to the market neatly arranged in their cane baskets. In this recipe, I have used red and green bell peppers and their sweetness is complemented by the warmth of roasted cumin seeds and the black pepper.

Preheat a small, heavy pan over a medium heat and add the cumin and black pepper. Stir until they begin to release their aroma, about 30–60 seconds, then remove from the pan. When the spices are cool, crush them.

In a small bowl, whisk the yogurt until smooth and stir in the salt. Reserve a little of the crushed spices to use as a garnish and stir the rest into the yogurt.

Add the bell peppers, mix well and transfer to a serving dish. Sprinkle the reserved spice mix on top and serve.

Serves 4–6

1 tsp cumin seeds

½ tsp black peppercorns

225 g/8 oz/1 cup whole milk plain yogurt

½ tsp salt, or to taste

1 red bell pepper, cut into bite-size pieces

1 green bell pepper, cut into bite-size pieces

My Secret
For an attractive presentation, slice off the top of two extra bell peppers and remove the seeds and the white pith. Then take a thin slice from the bottom of the peppers so that they sit securely on a plate. Fill with the prepared raita and serve. Later, I wash, chop and use the peppers in a stir-fry.

Tamatar ki Mithi Chutney

Sweet tomato chutney

Serves 4-6

2 tbsp sunflower or vegetable oil

½ tsp black mustard seeds

½ tsp onion seeds (kalonji)

500 g/1 lb tomatoes, skinned and chopped

50 g/2 oz/¼ cup light brown sugar

2 tsp ground cumin

½-1½ tsp chilli powder

1½ tsp salt, or to taste

50 g/2 oz/¼ cup seedless raisins

I remember being served this chutney at almost every wedding reception I went to with my mother and two sisters. As one of my sisters did not like it so much, I used to help her finish it by scooping it up with a piece of puri, deep-fried puffed bread.

In a medium saucepan, heat the oil over a medium heat. When hot but not smoking, add the mustard seeds. As soon as they begin to pop, throw in the onion seeds and then the tomatoes. Stir and reduce the heat slightly. Cover the pan and cook for 5 minutes.

Add the sugar, cumin, chilli powder and salt. Stir, cover again and cook for 5 minutes.

Add the raisins and cook, uncovered, for 9–10 minutes, stirring frequently over a medium-low heat until the chutney has thickened. Remove from the heat, cool and store in a dry airtight jar in the fridge. It will keep well for 3–4 weeks.

My Secret

Always make sure you use a dry spoon to remove the chutney from the jar. Any contact with moisture will reduce the life of the chutney.

Koshimbir
Raw vegetable salad

A classic recipe from South India in which the vegetables are cut into very small pieces and spiced lightly. The salad has to be made at least an hour before serving so that the vegetables can release their juices which then make a delicious, all-natural dressing.

In a coffee grinder or spice mill, grind the coconut until fine. In a mixing bowl, combine the coconut with all the ingredients except the oil, black mustard and cumin seeds. Mix well.

In a small steel ladle, heat the oil over a medium heat. When hot, add the black mustard and cumin seeds. Let them crackle for about 10 seconds, then pour the mixture over the salad. Mix thoroughly, cover the bowl and leave to stand for about 1 hour. Give the salad a good stir before serving.

Serves 4

25 g/1 oz/2 tbsp unsweetened desiccated coconut

125 g/4 oz/½ cup carrots, finely grated

125 g/4 oz/½ cup radishes, very finely chopped

225 g/8 oz/1 cup cucumber, peeled, deseeded and very finely chopped

1 small red onion, finely chopped

1 small green chilli, deseeded and finely chopped

2 tbsp coriander (cilantro) leaves, finely chopped

1½ tbsp lime juice

½ tsp salt, or to taste

1 tbsp sunflower or soya oil

½ tsp black mustard seeds

½ tsp cumin seeds

My Secret
The pungency of a chilli depends on the percentage of capsaicin (the heat-inducing element) present and this is more concentrated in the seeds. Removing the seeds reduces the pungency, but if you find you bite on a piece of hot chilli, do not reach for the water! My grandmother always gave us a spoonful of plain yogurt or a glass of cold milk to cool down. Trying to subdue the effect of capsaicin with water is like trying to mix oil and water.

Mewa ka Raita

Dry fruit and nuts in spiced yogurt

Serves 4

1 tbsp seedless raisins

1 tsp cumin seeds

½ tsp black peppercorns

225 g/8 oz/1 cup whole milk plain yogurt

6 ready-to-eat dried apricots, chopped

6 glacé cherries, halved, rinsed and dried

1 tbsp chopped raw cashew nuts

1 tbsp walnut pieces

½ tsp salt

½ tsp chilli powder or paprika

Every mouthful of this raita will delight you with its contrast in taste, texture and flavour. Raitas provide an essential balance to Indian meals and, though served at the side and consumed in small quantities, they are as important as the main dish. Yogurt is both cooling and easily digestible; cumin also aids digestion. This particular recipe comes from the royal repertoire, but you can use just about any fruit, fresh or dried, raw vegetable or salad ingredient to make a raita.

Soak the raisins in boiling water for 10 minutes to plump them up, then drain.

Preheat a small, heavy pan and dry-roast the cumin and peppercorns, stirring constantly, for 30–60 seconds or until they release their aroma. Cool, then crush them.

In a mixing bowl, whisk the yogurt. Add the drained raisins, apricots, cherries, cashews, walnuts and salt. Reserve a little of the crushed cumin and peppercorn mixture to use as a garnish and stir the remainder into the raita. Mix well, transfer to a serving dish and allow to stand for 30 minutes.

Sprinkle the reserved spice mixture and the chilli powder or paprika over the top of the raita before serving.

My Secret
You can use any combination of dried fruit and nuts as long as you make sure that you get a balance of sweet and sour in taste and crunchiness in texture.

Aam ki Chutney
Mango dip

This is not really a chutney, but a dip that is a delicious combination of mango purée, chilli and cumin. As you will probably guess from the ingredients, this is a pure invention on my part which, I hasten to add, is super-quick to make and is finger licking good! I have used plain yogurt and crème fraîche for the base, but you can vary this by choosing mayonnaise or unflavoured fromage frais instead of the crème fraîche.

In a small bowl, mix together all the ingredients except the cumin seeds. Put in the fridge to chill for 1–2 hours.

Meanwhile, in a small heavy pan, dry-roast the cumin seeds over a medium heat for 30–60 seconds, until fragrant. Remove and cool slightly, then crush them with a pestle or a rolling pin.

Just before serving, stir half the crushed cumin into the mango mixture and sprinkle the remainder on top as a garnish.

Serves 6–8

2 tbsp mango purée

1 tbsp fresh yogurt

1 tbsp crème fraîche

50 g/2 oz/¼ cup mango purée

25 g/1 oz/2 tbsp Greek yogurt

25 g/1 oz/2 tbsp crème fraîche

½ tsp chilli powder

½ tsp salt

1 tsp cumin seeds

My Secret
Buy a ripe fresh mango for a more savoury taste. Peel it then push the flesh through a sieve or purée it in a blender. Canned mangoes can be used if they are first drained thoroughly, but they will give a slightly sweet taste. Alternatively, you can buy canned mango purée from Indian shops.

Desserts

The secrets of sweet delights

Choosing the dessert is a skilful task in any cuisine. Once the starter and the main course have been selected, the dessert has to complement them – the wrong dessert is likely to upset the entire balance of the meal. Generally in India we opt for fresh fruit rather than a heavy dessert after a meal.

Although we have a fine range of sweets, they are more frequently eaten with tea and coffee, just like biscuits and cream cakes in the West. Sweets are also associated with festivals because they are considered to be 'foods of the Gods'. Festivals are times for sharing a common tie of religious and social beliefs.

Indian sweets tend to be quite heavy and rather sweet. In my experience, after a traditional Indian meal, people tend to prefer light, fruit-based desserts as their light and tangy flavours nicely offset the powerful aftertaste of spiced food.

However, a meal without a dessert, especially when you have a dinner party or cook for a special occasion, will seem incomplete. Here is a range of delicious and refreshing desserts which are perfect to round off a spicy meal.

The regional differences in sweets and desserts are quite significant as in the main cuisine. For instance, in the East, particularly in Bengal, a dazzling variey of milk based sweets are made. Renowned all over India, some of these are 'rasgollas' (milk balls flavoured with dardamomand rose water), 'Sandesh' (the soft and silky fudge-like sweetmeat made of fresh Indian cheese) and the ever popular 'Rasmalai' (milk balls smothered in a creamy saffron sauce). In the West, sweets come in the form of delicious laddus (dry balls) made of sesame seeds, rice and skinless mung beans. North India's most famous dessert is 'kulfi', which is popular all over India and abroad. Kulfi is traditionally made by gently simmering a large quantitiy of milk until it is reduced to half its original volume. Once cooled it is put into special conical shaped moulds (which explains their name) and frozen. Southern India's most famous dessert is 'Shrikand', made from strained yogurt and flavoured with saffron and cardamom.

Ale Belle

Coconut pancakes

This is a classic example of the mingling of Portuguese and Indian cultures in the cuisine of Goa. The batter for the pancake is more Western than Indian with the exception of the use of coconut milk. The pancakes are served with a sauce that is generally made of sweetened coconut milk. To cut the richness, I have used lime juice and the zest of limes and oranges.

To make the pancakes, in a mixing bowl, blend the coconut with 300 ml/½ pint/1¼ cups of boiling water and add the butter. Stir until the butter has melted then set aside to cool completely.

Gradually stir the beaten eggs into the coconut mixture. Sieve the flour into a separate bowl and mix in the nutmeg and salt. Add 1 tablespoon of the dry ingredients at a time to the coconut mixture, beating with a whisk between each addition. Alternatively, blend all the ingredients together in a blender or food processor. Let the batter stand for 20–25 minutes before cooking.

In a 15–18 cm/6–7 in diameter frying pan (preferably non-stick) heat 1 teaspoon of oil over a medium heat. Using a ladle large enough to hold 4 tablespoons of the batter, add some batter to the pan and spread it round the base quickly. Allow to cook for 30 seconds, then flip and cook for 30 seconds. Fold the pancake into a triangle and transfer to an ovenproof plate. Repeat with the remaining batter and keep the pancakes in a warm oven while you make the sauce.

Place the sugar in a saucepan with 300 ml/½ pint/1¼ cups of water. Bring it to the boil and reduce the heat to medium. Add the remaining sauce ingredients except the coconut. Cook for 6–7 minutes, then add the coconut, reduce the heat to low and simmer for 4–5 minutes. Remove from the heat. Place 2 pancakes per person on individual serving plates and divide the sauce equally

.

Serves 4

For the pancakes:

90 g/3 oz/⅓ cup grated creamed coconut

2 tbsp butter

2 medium eggs, beaten

125 g/4 oz/¾ cup self-raising flour

½ tsp ground nutmeg

a pinch of salt

sunflower or soya oil, for frying

For the sauce:

90 g/3½ oz/⅓ cup caster sugar

2 tbsp raw cashews, broken

1½ tbsp seedless raisins

finely grated zest and juice of 1 lime

finely grated zest of 1 orange

90 g/3 oz/1⅓ cup grated creamed coconut

My Secret
For an extra special treat, stir in 4 tablespoons Malibu to the sauce just before serving. Also for an enhanced flavour, use freshly grated nutmeg rather than pre-ground. As with all whole spices, the essential oil in the nutmeg is released only when it is ground or grated, adding loads of flavour to your food.

Chocolate Kulfi with Mandarin Sauce

Chocolate ice cream with mandarin sauce

Makes 10–12

oil, for brushing

410 ml/13 fl oz/1⅔ cups evaporated milk

300 ml/½ pint/1¼ cups double (heavy) cream

5 tbsp caster (superfine) sugar

25 g/1 oz/2 tbsp ground almonds

150 g/5 oz/1 cup plain (semi-sweet) chocolate

1 tsp ground cinnamon

For the sauce:

2 x 300 g/10 ½oz cans mandarin segments in syrup

1½ tbsp arrowroot

2 tbsp Cointreau, Grand Marnier or other orange liqueur

1 tbsp toasted flaked almonds

Kulfi is described as the Indian ice cream though it has a harder and denser texture than Western versions. During the blazing Indian summer, an ice-cold kulfi is highly inviting as well as nourishing. There were always kulfiwallas (kulfi sellers) who would bring it to the door. The kulfi moulds were carefully arranged in traditional wooden containers filled with a mixture of ice and salt. The wood as well as the salt prevented the ice from melting too quickly and kept the kulfi at the required temperature. This was a poor man's ingenious version of a portable freezer. Kulfi moulds can be bought from Asian stores, but small jelly moulds or ice lolly (popsicle) moulds are quite adequate.

Lightly brush a heavy saucepan with oil. Add the evaporated milk, cream, sugar and ground almonds, mix well and place over a low heat. Bring slowly to a gentle simmer, stirring frequently. Remove from the heat and let cool, covered with a moist cloth.

Break up the chocolate as necessary and place in a heatproof bowl over a pan of simmering water. When melted, stir the chocolate and cinnamon into the milk mixture and beat until well blended. Put the mixture into moulds of your choice and freeze for 7–8 hours.

To make the sauce, purée the mandarin segments in a blender. Transfer to a saucepan and heat until the mixture begins to bubble. In a small bowl, blend the arrowroot with a little water and stir into the mandarin purée. Cook gently until the sauce has thickened, remove from the heat and leave to cool. Stir the liqueur into the sauce then chill in a covered container.

Unmould the frozen kulfi onto a serving plate and surround it with the mandarin sauce. Top with the toasted almonds and serve.

My Secrets

Brushing the saucepan with oil before heating the milk prevents the milk sticking to the bottom of the pan.

It s best to cover the cooked milk mixture with a moist cloth such as a clean tea towel in order to prevent a skin forming as it cools.

Aam ka Halwa
Soft mango fudge

Instead of a dessert, you can serve this delicious soft fudge as a sweetmeat with some coffee. You can buy sweetened mango purée from Indian stores, but canned mango slices can be puréed and used instead.

Put the sugar into a saucepan with 300 ml/½ pint/1¼ cups water. Place over a high heat and stir until the sugar has dissolved. Stir in the saffron strands and set aside.

In a heavy sauté pan or frying pan, melt the ghee or butter over a low heat and add the semolina and cashews. Cook for 5–6 minutes, stirring frequently, then add the ground almonds. Continue cooking and stirring for 3–4 minutes or until the mixture is light brown and a toasted aroma is released.

Mix the mango purée and rose water together and add them to the sugar syrup. Pour the mixture into the semolina and stir over a low heat for 3–4 minutes or until it thickens and stops sticking to the bottom and sides of the pan.

Using a metal spoon, spread the mixture onto a greased plate to a thickness of about 1 cm/½ in. Press the sides inwards with a knife to form a large square. Leave to cool, then cut into 2.5 cm/1 in squares.

Top each square with 1–2 pistachios and gently press them into the surface to secure. Chill before serving.

Serves 8

125 g/4 oz/½ cup caster (superfine) sugar

a large pinch of saffron strands, pounded

125 g/4 oz/½ cup ghee or unsalted butter, plus extra for greasing

125 g/4 oz/½ cup semolina

50 g/2 oz/¼ cup raw cashews, chopped

125 g/4 oz/½ cup ground almonds

300 ml/½ pint/1¼ cups sweetened mango purée or 2 x 400g/14 oz cans sliced mango, drained and puréed

2 tbsp rose water

1½ tbsp shelled pistachio nuts, lightly toasted

My Secret
Indian housewives would offer this sweet with tea and coffee when friends drop in. Theirs would have a more intense mango flavour as they would only use fresh ripe mango and purée it with a little water.

Khubani ka Mitha

Apricot dessert

Serves 4–6

500 g/1 lb/3⅓ cups ready-to-eat dried apricots

125 g/4 oz/½ cup caster (superfine) sugar

2–3 tbsp shelled, raw pistachio nuts

lightly whipped double (heavy) cream, to serve

'Simplicity' could easily be an alternative name for this delightful recipe. In the princely southern state of Hyderabad, where this luscious golden dessert was created, the kernel inside the hard shell of the apricot stone is removed and used to decorate the dessert. I have opted to use dried apricots and pistachio nuts to create a striking garnish.

Put the apricots into a saucepan with 750 ml/1¼ pints/3 cups of water and bring to the boil. Reduce the heat to low, cover the pan and simmer for 15 minutes or until the apricots are soft, stirring at least twice during cooking.

Remove half the apricots with a slotted spoon and set aside. Purée the remainder along with their cooking juices and return the purée to the saucepan. Add the whole apricots and the sugar. Cook gently for 3–4 minutes, remove from the heat and let cool for about 30 minutes.

Meanwhile, toast the pistachio nuts under a preheated low grill (broiler) for 2–3 minutes or in a moderate oven for about 5 minutes. Cool them for a few minutes and crush lightly with a rolling pin.

Put the apricot mixture in individual serving plates and sprinkle with the crushed pistachio nuts. Serve with the whipped cream.

My Secrets

For a luxurious touch, add 2–3 tablespoons of orange-flavoured liqueur such as Cointreau or Drambuie to the whipped cream.

When in season, use fresh apricots which will always produce a more luscious taste and flavour. Cover the apricots in boiling water for a few minutes, for easy peeling of the skin

Ananas aur Nariyal ka Mitha

Pineapple and coconut dessert

Pineapple was first brought to India from South America and it is now grown extensively in the hilly North and North Eastern Terrain. Its bright golden colour, together with the sweet, juicy flesh, seem to be a natural partner for rich yet mellow coconut milk.

Strain the canned pineapple and reserve the juice. You should have 150 ml/5 fl oz/⅔ cup – if not, add water to make up the difference.

Place the coconut in a small saucepan with 300 ml/½ pint/1¼ cups of water. Sprinkle the gelatine on top and heat very gently until the gelatine has dissolved. Remove the pan from the heat and add the sugar, lemon zest and juice. Stir until dissolved.

Add the crushed pineapple and leave to cool. Meanwhile, whip the cream. When the pineapple mixture is cool, stir in the brandy, if using, then fold in the whipped cream. Rinse out one large or several individual moulds with cold water. Pour in the pineapple cream and refrigerate for 5–6 hours.

To turn out, dip the mould or moulds in hot water for 10–15 seconds and invert the dessert onto a serving plate. Sprinkle the ground cinnamon on top and arrange a few mandarin segments round the edges. Sprinkle the Grenadine randomly over the mandarin and serve the dessert.

Serves 6

1 x 400 g/14 oz can crushed pineapple in juice

100 g/3½ oz/⅓ cup creamed coconut, cut into small pieces

1 sachet (11g/½oz) gelatine

125–150 g/4–5 oz/⅓–½ cup caster (superfine) sugar

finely grated zest of 1 lemon, plus 1 tbsp juice

2 tbsp brandy (optional)

150 ml/5 fl oz/⅔ cup double (heavy) cream

½ tsp ground cinnamon

a few mandarin orange segments in juice, drained

a few drops of Grenadine

My Secret

You could create a delicious variation by thickening the mandarin juice with 1 tablespoon of ground arrowroot blended with a little cold water. Heat gently until thickened and spoon it around the dessert, then serve with the mandarin segments and the grenadine as above.

Fresh coconut milk will produce an infinitely better taste. It's easy to make this in as electric blender. Simply purée the fresh coconut with a little water to facilitate blade movement. Strain through a muslin cloth, squeezing out every drop.

Ananas ka Muzaffar

Pineapple and rice dessert

Serves 4–6

175 g/6 oz/¾ cup basmati rice

4 tbsp ghee or unsalted butter, plus extra for greasing

25 g/1 oz/1½ tbsp seedless raisins

25 g/1 oz/1½ tbsp flaked almonds

5 green cardamom pods, bruised

5 cloves

4 x 1 cm/½ in sticks cinnamon

a large pinch of saffron strands, pounded

225 g/8 oz/1 cup cubed fresh pineapple, or ½ medium pineapple, peeled and cubed

150–175 g/5–6 oz/ ⅔–¾ cup) caster (superfine) sugar

With the exotic perfume and delicious golden flesh of pineapple, the seductive fragrance and slender, silky grains of basmati rice bathed in evocatively rich saffron, this is ambrosia in all its glory!

Wash the rice in several changes of water and leave to drain. In a heavy saucepan, melt the ghee or butter over a low heat and fry the raisins until they swell. Remove with a slotted spoon and drain on absorbent paper. Next, fry the almonds until light brown then remove and drain as above.

In the remaining oil, fry the cardamom, cloves and cinnamon gently for 25–30 seconds. Add the rice, increase the heat slightly and stir-fry the rice for 2–3 minutes.

Add the saffron and 300 ml/½ pint /1¼ cups of lukewarm water. Bring it to the boil and cook for 2 minutes, then reduce the heat to low. Continue cooking, uncovered, for 2–3 minutes until the surface water has been absorbed. Remove the pan from the heat.

Preheat the oven to 170°C/325°F/Gas 3. Brush the sides and the bottom of an ovenproof casserole with a little butter. Place one-third of the rice on it. Cover with one-third of the pineapple pieces and sprinkle one-third of the sugar evenly over the top. Repeat until you have used up all the rice, pineapple and sugar.

Soak a piece of greaseproof paper in water and crumple it. Place it loosely over the top of the dessert. Cover the paper loosely with a crumpled piece of foil, but seal the edges by pressing them round the entire rim of the dish. Put the lid on and bake in the centre of the oven for 35–40 minutes. When done, switch off the oven and leave the rice in it for 10–15 minutes.

Reserve a little of the fried raisins and nuts to decorate before serving and carefully mix the remainder into the rice. Serve.

My Secrets

For convenience you could use canned pineapple in natural juice if you drain it well first.

If you buy a fresh pineapple, you could use the other half to tenderise inexpensive cuts of meat. The special enzyme in pineapple is very effective in breaking down the muscle fibres and allows flavourings to penetrate deeper. Purée the pineapple and use approximately 75 g/2½ oz per 700 g/1½ lb of meat.

Phal ka Murabba

Punch jelly

A deliciously intoxicating lemon-flavoured jelly laced with brandy and port, this recipe comes from the exciting repertoire created during the days of the British Raj. I like to serve it with plenty of fresh exotic fruits such as papaya, mango, pomegranate and lychees.

In a large saucepan, place the brandy, port, sugar, cinnamon, allspice, cloves and 125 ml/4 fl oz/½ cup of water. Bring to the boil, cover and simmer for 5 minutes.

Cut the jelly into cubes and add to the spiced liquid. Stir until dissolved, then cover and set aside for 10–15 minutes.

Strain the spiced punch into a bowl and stand the bowl in iced water. When the mixture is lukewarm, stir in the milk.

In a large mixing bowl, whisk the cream until it is thick but not stiff. Gradually add the punch while still whisking.

Rinse out a 600 ml/1 pint/2½ cup ring mould or other decorative mould with cold water and pour in the punch-flavoured cream. Refrigerate for 5–6 hours or until set. Turn out onto a serving plate and decorate with fruits of your choice.

Serves 6

125 ml/4 fl oz/½ cup brandy

4 tbsp port wine

50 g/2 oz/¼ cup caster (superfine) sugar

5 cm/2 in stick cinnamon, broken

135 g/4 oz/½ cup whole allspice

6 cloves

1 packet lemon-flavoured jelly cubes

150 ml/5 fl oz/⅔ cup whole milk

150 ml /5 fl oz/⅔ cup double (heavy) cream

fresh fruit, to decorate

My Secret
I like to set this dessert in a ring mould and fill the centre with a colourful selection of exotic fruits. Use a plain serving plate and sprinkle a mixture of cocoa powder and icing (confectioner's) sugar around the turned out jelly as well as over it. If you rinse your serving plate with cold water first, it will be easier to move the mould if it is not exactly in the centre of the plate. Wipe the edges dry before sprinkling with cocoa powder and icing (confectioner's) sugar.

Stockists and Suppliers of Indian Ingredients

T & G Woodware have all the spices in airtight jars fined with ceramic crushgrind spice mills. This means freshly ground spices every time with superb flavours. They also stock Mridula Baljekar's own spice blends complete with the spice mills. These are Korma Mix, Chicken Tikka Mix, Dhansak Mix and Garam Masala Mix. These are available in all major department stores and speciality kitchen equipment shops. For information on your nearest stockist please telephone:
+44 1275 841841
or fax: +44 1275 841800

AVON
Bart Spices Ltd
York Road
Bedminster
Bristol B53 4AD
(Also mail order service)
Tel: +44 117 977 3474
Fax: +44 117 972 0216

BERKSHIRE
Medina Stores
27 Debeauvoir Road
Reading
Berkshire RG I 5NR
Tel: +44 118 987 1171

EDINBURGH
Nastiuks (wholesaler)
Nine Mile Burn Garage
Nine Mile Burn
A702
South of Edinburgh
Midlothian EH26 9LT
Tel: +44 1968 679 333

GLASGOW
Oriental Food Stores
303–5 Great Western Road
Glasgow G4 9115
Tel: +44 141 334 8133

HUMBERSIDE
Indian and Continental Food Stores
69 Princess Avenue
Hull HUS 3QN
Tel: +44 1482 346 915

LONDON
Dadu's Limited
190-198 Upper Tooting Road
London SWI7 7EW.
Tel: +44 181 672 4984

The Clifton Sweetmart
118 Brick Lane
London EI
Tel: +44 171 247 5811

Asian Food Centre
544 Harrow Road
Maida Vale
London W9 3GG.
Tel: +44 181 960 3751

MIDDLESEX
Asian Food Centre
175–77 Staines Road
Hounslow
Middx TW3 3JB
Tel: +44 181 570 7346

100–200 Ealing Road,
Wembley
This address has shops such as Dadoos with a comprehensive range of Indian foods and ingredients.

Dadoos
off Ealing Road (100 yards away)
Wembley (near Alperton Bus Station)

SURREY
Spicyfoods Cash and Carry
460 London Road
Croydon
Surrey CR0 2SS.
Tel: +44 181 684 9844

Atif's Superstore
103 Walton Road
Woking
Surrey GU2 I 5DW
Tel: +44 1483 762 774

YORKSHIRE
Bhullar Brothers Ltd
44 Springwood Street
Huddersfield
W Yorkshire HD1 4BE
Tel: +44 1484 531 607

Index

aniseed 11
apricot dessert 152
asafoetida (hing) 11
aubergines:
  aubergine and chickpea
    curry 22
  spiced baked aubergine 51

beetroot bread 129
beetroot with lamb 74
bread: 32, 118
  beetroot bread 129
  bread with spiced eggs 133
  creamy rich bread 128
  deep-fried puffed bread 126
  deep-fried puffed bread with
    spinach 130
  fenugreek flat bread 132
  garlic bread 131
  milk bread 127
  naan with spicy meat
    filling 134–5

carrot and spinach in spiced
  yogurt 139
cheese, Indian (paneer) 9
  marinated pan-fried strips of
    Indian cheese 93
  pilau rice with peas and
    Indian cheese 124
chickpea and aubergine
  curry 22
chillies: 8
  potatoes with ginger and
    chillies 24
  vegetables with garlic and
    chillies 23
chocolate ice cream with
  mandarin sauce 150

chutney: 138
  mango dip 145
  mint and onion chutney 140
  sweet tomato chutney 142
coconut:
  coconut and pineapple
    dessert 153
  coconut kebabs 94
  coconut pancakes 149
cooking utensils 15, 32, 48,
  66, 106
crab cakes 113
cumin, black (shahi jeera) 11
cumin-flavoured rice 120
curry:
  aubergine and chickpea
    curry 22
  curry leaves 11
  meat and potato curry with
    hot oil seasoning 29

deep-frying 106

eggs:
  bread with spiced eggs 133
  hard boiled eggs encased
    in spiced lamb 99

fenugreek: 11
  fenugreek flat bread 132
  vegetables with
    fenugreek 25
fish:
  Amritsar-style fish 112
  fish baked in an aromatic
    sauce 58
  fish in aromatic tomato
    sauce 27
  fish korma 68

fish with stir-fried spices 38
five-spice mix: 13
  red lentils with five-spice
    seasoning 19
flour 8, 106, 118
freezing 14
fruit, dried:
  dry fruit and nuts in spiced
    yogurt 144
  dry fruit pilau 123

garlic: 8
  garlic bread 131
  vegetables with garlic and
    chillies 23
ghee 9, 18
ginger: 8
  potatoes with ginger and
    chillies 24

herbs 9, 138

ice cream: chocolate ice
  cream with mandarin
    sauce 150

jelly, punch 155

kebabs: 78, 92
  chicken kebabs in a rich red
    sauce 96
  coconut kebabs 94
  minced lamb or beef
    kebab 98
korma cooking 66

lamb with mango 39
lentils:
  fried split yellow lentils 37

lentils with prawns 28
red lentils with five-spice
    seasoning 19
spiced red lentils 21
spiced whole red lentils 20

mango:
  mango dip 145
  mango with lamb 39
  soft mango fudge 151
marrow:
  spiced marrow 34
  stuffed whole marrow 54–5
meat: 66
  Goan spicy roast pork 89
  hard boiled eggs encased
      in spiced lamb 99
  heavenly korma 73
  lamb with beetroot 74
  lamb with mango 39
  marinated lamb's liver 103
  meat and potato curry with
      hot oil seasoning 29
  meat with stir-fried
      spices 45
  minced lamb or beef
      kebab 98
  minced meat with
      orange 40
  mini meatballs 115
  naan with spicy meat
      filling 134–5
  Peshawar-style skewered
      lamb 102
  pilau rice with spiced
      lamb 125
  rice steamed with aromatic
      lamb 62–3
  royal braised lamb 75

slow-cooked lamb
    shanks 59
slow-cooked lamb with
    turnips 60–1
spiced liver 44
spiced minced lamb
    patties 100–1
spicy minced hare 41
stir-fried meatballs 42–3
tandoori lamb chops 88
mint and onion chutney 140

nuts:
  dry fruit and nuts in spiced
      yogurt 144
  spiced almonds and
      cashews 108

oil: 9, 18, 106
  meat and potato curry with
      hot oil seasoning 29
  tomatoes with hot oil
      seasoning 26
okra with onions 33
onions: 8
  mint and onion chutney 140
  okra with onions 33
  onion seeds 11
orange with minced meat 40

peas:
  aubergine and chickpea
      curry 22
  pilau rice with peas and
      Indian cheese 124
peppers:
  batter-fried sweet pepper
      rings 110
  sweet peppers in spiced

yogurt 141
pineapple:
  pineapple and coconut
      dessert 153
  pineapple and rice
      dessert 154
poppy seeds, white (khas
      khas) 11
  potatoes with poppy
      seeds 36
potatoes:
  meat and potato curry with
      hot oil seasoning 29
  potatoes with ginger and
      chillies 24
  potatoes with poppy
      seeds 36
  spiced baked potatoes 50
  spiced potato cakes 111
  spicy potato fritters 109
  spinach with potatoes 52
  tandoori potatoes 81
poultry:
  chicken kebabs in a rich red
      sauce 96
  Goan spiced chicken 84
  grilled turkey breast with
      sesame seeds 83
  korma of stuffed whole
      chicken 70–1
  marinated chicken
      drumsticks 97
  spicy chicken fritters 114
  stuffed quails 56–7
  tandoori chicken with green
      spice mix 85
  tandoori-style whole guinea
      fowl 86–7
  white chicken korma 72

prawns:
  prawn korma 69
  prawns with lentils 28
  tandoori king prawns 82
punch jelly 155

rice: 10, 32, 118
  cumin-flavoured rice 120
  dry fruit pilau 123
  mint and coriander rice 122
  pilau rice with peas and
          Indian cheese 124
  pilau rice with spiced
          lamb 125
  pineapple and rice
          dessert 154
  plain pilau rice 119
  rice steamed with aromatic
          lamb 62–3
  saffron pilau 121

salad, raw vegetable 143
shellfish:
  crab cakes 113
  lentils with prawns 28
  prawn korma 69
  tandoori king prawns 82
spices 12–13, 18, 32
spinach:
  carrot and spinach in
          spiced yogurt 139
  deep-fried puffed bread with
          spinach 130
  spinach with potatoes 52
steam cooking 48
stir-frying 32
stock 10
sweet peppers in spiced
          yogurt 141

tamarind 10
tandoori cooking 78
tomatoes:
  fish in aromatic tomato
          sauce 27
  stuffed tomatoes 53
  sweet tomato chutney 142
  tomatoes with hot oil
          seasoning 26
turnips:
  slow cooked lamb with
          turnips 60–1
  spiced turnip puree 35

vegetables:
  aubergine and chickpea
          curry 22
  baby corn fritters 107
  batter-fried sweet pepper
          rings 110
  okra with onions 33
  pilau rice with peas and
          Indian cheese 124
  raw vegetable salad 143
  spiced marrow 34
  spiced steamed
          vegetables 49
  spiced turnip puree 35
  stuffed whole marrow 54-5
  tandoori cauliflower 80
  tandoori pumpkin 79
  vegetable korma 67
  vegetables with
          fenugreek 25
  vegetables with garlic and
          chillies 23
  vegetarian flat cakes 95

water 10, 32

yogurt:
  carrot and spinach in
          spiced yogurt 139
  dry fruit and nuts in spiced
          yogurt 144
  sweet peppers in spiced
          yogurt 141

Acknowledgements

I am grateful to Karim's Restaurant in Old Delhi, India for their generosity in opening the door to the secrets of the exquisite Moghul cooking.

My sincere thanks to Outdoor Chef for the fabulous barbecue which proved invaluable in my experiment in cooking the tandoori dishes.

The job of chopping, mixing and blending was made infinitely easier by Magi mix. Thank you Pam Bewley.

My thanks to The Solo Sea Salt Company for providing me with low sodium sea salt which can be used in all the recipes with superb flavour profiles.

A big 'thank you' to T & G Woodware for providing me with superb quality kitchen tools, including chopping boards and skewers! But, best of all, the fabulous spice mills which filled my kitchen with fresh aroma every time I tested the recipes!

Sincere thanks to Rucker & Slann for sending me the prime quality spices which were a delight to work with.

Last, but not least, loving thanks to my two daughters, Maneesha and Sneha for their enthusiasm in sharing the secrets of fine Indian cooking which I learnt all those years ago from their grandmother and great grandmother!